W9-AUY-139

Foster Care

Foster Care

Nancy Millichap Davies

The *Changing* Family

FRANKLIN WATTS
New York   Chicago   London   Toronto   Sydney

3 3113 01383 1906

Photographs copyright ©: Archive Photos, NYC: p. 1; The Bettmann Archive: pp. 2, 4, 5; St. Joseph Museum, St. Joseph, Missouri: p. 3 top; The Library of Congress: p.3 bottom; UNICEF Photos: pp. 6 (Marcus Halevi), 7 top (Bill Hetzer); UN Photos: p. 7 bottom (Kevin Bubriski); C.S.R. Inc.: p. 8; Gamma-Liaison: pp. 9 (Stephen Ferry), 10 (Cynthia Johnson), 11 (Steve Hamblin), 12 (Yvonne Hemsey), 14 (Bard Wrisley); Photo Researchers, Inc.: pp. 13 (Barbara Rios), 15 (Blair Seitz), 16 (Day Williams).

Library of Congress Cataloging-in-Publication Data

Davies, Nancy Millichap.
Foster care / Nancy Millichap Davies.
p.   cm. — (The Changing family)
Includes bibliographical references and index.
ISBN 0-531-11081-8
1. Foster home care—United States.   I. Title.   II. Series:
Changing family (New York, N.Y.)
HV881.D37   1994
362.7'33'0973—dc20   93-23237   CIP   AC

For Albert Edward Millichap

Contents

1
What is
Foster Care?
11

2
The History of
Foster Care
19

3
Why Children
Enter Care
28

4
Life in
Foster Homes
37

5
Foster Parents
46

6
Caseworkers
53

7
Foster Care
Laws
61

8
Leaving
Foster Care
69

9
Foster Care
Controversies
76

10
Alternatives to
Foster Care
84

Source Notes
92

Bibliography
105

Index
110

Foster Care

1 What Is Foster Care?

In Ruthie's pretty room, full of toys and sunlight, she's just starting to talk. The woman she calls "Mama" is not the one who gave birth to her eleven months ago. Instead, she's a foster parent who brought Ruthie home as a newborn to her bright, spacious apartment above a California beach. Ruthie's biological mother was suffering from a severe episode of mental illness when her daughter was born, but has now been released from the mental hospital. She does not have a job yet, but she wants her baby daughter to live with her. Ruthie's foster mother had hoped to adopt her, and she is heartsick.

Kara is a small girl for her four years, with dark eyes that seem too big for her face. Until last month, she and her three half-brothers lived in a Chicago housing project. Most of the time, their mother was away from the apartment. Sometimes, when she did come home, she was under the influence of street drugs and didn't give Kara and her brothers much attention then. Kara's grandmother lived in a nearby building in the same project. She checked on the children every morning and spent most evenings with them. Last winter, though, the grandmother became seriously ill and had to go into the hospital. A woman from the Cook County child welfare agency came to tell Kara and her brothers that they would be entering foster care. Kara now lives with a couple who have two daughters and a son of their own, and two other foster children in addition to Kara. Kara feels sad and confused. She misses her brothers. She wonders where her mother and grandmother are.

Luis is a fifth-grader in Portland, Oregon. For the first half of this school year, he was absent more than any other student in his class. When he did make it to school, he rarely talked. No one was sure where he lived, but wherever it was, he seemed to have a lot of accidents. He had bruises or bandages on his arms and legs almost all the time. One day he came to school with his arm in a sling made from an old dish towel. His teacher sent him to the nurse, who found that his arm was broken. Although he did not want to explain what happened, he finally told the guidance counselor that his new father had thrown him against a wall. That afternoon, when the other children went home, the counselor took Luis to a social service office in downtown Portland. His mother was there, crying. She said that Luis made a lot of mess around the house, and it bothered her new husband who was not used to children. After a long discussion, Luis's mother signed some papers. She and the social worker told Luis he'd be going to stay with another family for a while. He has spent the last four months living in a different part of the city with a foster mother. She's a single parent with a boy of her own who's ten, just like Luis. Once every two weeks, the child welfare department social worker assigned to the case picks Luis up on a Saturday morning. She takes him to the downtown office of the agency, where he sees his mother for an hour. The room is noisy, full of other children visiting with their parents. One Saturday, Luis's mother says, "Dad's had a lot of counseling. He's ready to have you come home again." Luis will be returning to live with his mom and her husband next week. He wants to go, but he's still afraid.

When Doug was fourteen, he and his mom moved from an apartment in Brooklyn to a house in the Bronx, where her new boyfriend lived. (Doug doesn't remember his real dad, and his mother never talks about him.) The boyfriend and Doug had arguments about Doug's grades, his appearance, and the hours he was keeping. Doug started spending most of his time back in his old neighborhood with boys his age who didn't go home much either. With them, he started drinking, using street drugs, and breaking into cars. When he and several friends were held for questioning by the police, his mother's boyfriend told her to choose between Doug and him. She contacted the city child welfare department to say that she just couldn't handle her son. She asked about having Doug placed in a foster home "just until he gets straightened out." He's been in two foster homes in the seven months since then. When the foster parents he's staying with now find out that he is stealing money from his foster mother's handbag, he expects he'll be moving on again. The social worker he meets with every other week has told him that he'll have to go into a group home the next time.

The names in these stories have been changed, but stories like these happen every day. About 340,000 young people were in foster care in the United States in 1991,[1] up from 251,000 in care in 1983.[2] The *Encyclopedia of Social Work* defines foster care as full-time, substitute care of children outside their own homes by caretakers other than a child's biological parents, who may be related or unrelated adults.

Reasons for Foster Care

To *foster* means to bring up with care. Parents do just that for children, in an ideal world. But children like Kara, Luis, and Doug live in places that are far from ideal. A large number of the children placed in care are being protected from abuse, like Luis. An even larger group have parents who are judged to be neglecting them, like Kara's mother, or who are incapable of caring for them, like Ruthie's mother. A much smaller number, like Doug, are in trouble with the law.[3]

Even though there are many valid reasons for placing children and adolescents in foster care, it is always a second-best substitute. Americans, like people in all societies throughout the world, see life in one's own family with one's own parents as a fundamental fact of life.[4] No matter how difficult their lives with their own parents may be, children cannot avoid being deeply unsettled by the transfer from their "real" home to a foster home. First, there is the trauma of separation from the people the child knows best. Second, both foster children and foster parents remain aware that they are only temporarily a family, and it is hard for trust to develop between them, especially if the child has been moved from home to home several times. Trust is most likely to develop in situations where a foster child stays with the same foster parents for a long time, or if the foster family adopts the child. Foster care is by definition temporary, however, and social service workers try hard to keep placements as brief as possible. No matter how long a child is in foster care, he or she is available for adoption only if the child's biological parents give up their parental rights or the Court terminates their parental rights over the parents' objections. Most biological parents don't give up their rights willingly. Also, not all foster care providers are interested in adopting children.

How the System Works

Foster care has been described as "drastic social surgery."[5] All the adults involved in making choices about foster care—biological parents, foster parents, and social welfare workers—realize that the decision to place children in care is gravely important. In addition to the psychological effects on the child and the child's biological

14

parents, entering care represents a significant change in the child's position legally. When children are placed in foster care, a government social welfare agency takes over legal custody in place of the birth parent or parents.[6] Often, the parents and the child welfare agencies that handle foster care placements do not see eye to eye about when, or whether, this step is necessary. If an agency can show that children have been maltreated, the children may be placed in foster care by court order without their parents' agreement.

Once a child has been removed from home and placed in foster care, there are additional serious questions to answer. How long will the child remain in care? While he or she is living away from home, will there be visits with the natural parents? How often? Where will the parent or parents visit with their child, and how will they get there? What steps do the parents need to take before the family can be reunited, that is, before the child returns home? How will the child welfare agency or the court recognize that these steps have been taken? If it looks as though the child will never be able to return home, is adoption a possibility? If adoption is not a possibility, what kind of long-term arrangement will best suit the child?

Foster care is intended to be a temporary living arrangement. Ideally, while parents and child are apart, the parents solve their family problems with the help of a caseworker, and the child returns home to an improved family life. This does happen in some cases. For at least half the children who are placed, foster care is a short-term experience. In one study, just over 50 percent of the children who were placed in foster care returned home within six months.[7] But about a quarter of the children in the same study had been in foster care for at least two years. Many of the children who enter care never live with their original parents again. Children deserve something better.

Biological and Psychological Parents

At birth, a child naturally enters the home of his or her biological parents. Being a parent involves more than simply giving birth to a child, however. One recent theory that has influenced child welfare planning is that of the *psychological parent*. This psychological parent is the person who not only takes care of the child's physical needs, but also interacts with the child, is a companion to the child on a day-to-day basis, and meets the child's need for affection and feeling wanted. This psychological parent is, in the child's mind, that child's parent, whether he or she is related by blood or not. The biological parents become the psychological parents unless other adults take on that role.

If the child spends a long time in foster care, foster parents may become the psychological parents. This is especially likely to happen if the child is placed in care as an infant, or when very young. Some social welfare planners believe that the most important thing society can do for a child is to make sure that he or she remains with a psychological parent.[8] They say that providing a child with the security of living with a psychological parent is even more important than are the rights of biological parents.

Permanency Planning

Others who are interested in child welfare have a different way of describing the importance of security for children. They think the foster care system should fix its sights on finding every child a permanent home. This idea is known as *permanency planning*. It became a United States law in 1980 when Congress passed House Bill 96–272, the Adoption Assistance and Child Welfare Reform Act.[9] According to this law, every child has the right to a permanent family setting. The law requires that child welfare agencies make a definite plan for a child's future when they take the child into care. This plan should identify a specific permanent living arrangement as the goal for the child. It should also spell out the steps that the agency's caseworkers and the child's parents will take so that the child is able to live in that permanent home within some reasonable period of time.

According to PL 96–272, a decision about a child's permanent home should be made by the time the child has been in foster care for eighteen months.[10] There are, in most cases, two possibilities for a permanent home. First, the child may return to his or her parents. Second, the parents may give up their parental rights. Once they do, the child is free to be adopted by another family. The first possibility occurs in many cases. But the second alternative, legal adoption by a different family, doesn't happen very often. Terminating parents' rights when they do not want to give up their parental rights requires careful judgment and extensive time in court. Social welfare personnel are often working with several dozen children at once. Courts are crowded, too, and many judges are not comfortable with the idea of terminating parental rights, even in clear cases of abuse and neglect.

When the child cannot return home but the courts will not terminate the parental rights of the child's biological parents, there is a third alternative. Long-term foster care can be an option if it is planned rather than if, as happens all too often, children "drift" from one short-term placement to another. According to one estimate, a child placed in foster care has less than a 50 percent chance of experiencing only a single placement.[11]

When long-term foster placements work out as social welfare planners hope they will, children who are not free for adoption have a single, stable placement with one family that lasts until they become independent adults. In some cases, this does happen. One study of young adults who had been in foster care for at least five years and who had left foster care at age eighteen found that 90 percent were still in touch with their foster families, and 75 percent felt close to them four or five years after they had left foster care. Only 25 percent of the same young adults were in regular touch with their original kin.[12] Foster parents, in the majority of these cases, appear to have become the psychological parents of these young adults. But it is unusual today for foster children to be placed with just one family.

The Ruthies, Karas, Luises, and Dougs whose families are struggling with emotional, financial, and social problems are seriously at risk. They are going through experiences that may do lasting damage to their potential as humans. Foster care placements, while offering an alternative to children whose families are in trouble, are far from a "cure-all." It is all too easy for human concerns to be diminished within the foster care system, with its maze of laws and its mountains of paperwork. For many children, the system works as it should, providing temporary refuge and, eventually, permanent security. For many others, it becomes not a solution but instead part of the problem. It is easy to look at foster care statistics and become discouraged. Yet Trudy Festinger's 1983 study of New York young adults who had spent not just a few weeks or months, but much of their youth in foster care, concluded that they were more similar to than different from others of their age.[13] For at least some of the children it attempts to help, the foster care system is not the disastrous mess that newspaper headlines frequently suggest.

2 The History of Foster Care

The first kind of foster care that emerged in the United States was called *indenture*. From the early days of the British colonies through the late 1800s, children who had no homes were legally assigned, or indentured, to people willing to take them. Indentured servants then worked for these people until they reached a certain age. Sometimes they were servants, sometimes farm hands, and sometimes apprentices in the workshops of craftsmen. The indentured child received no pay but did get food, clothing, a place to live and, often, vocational training. When the time of indenture was over, usually at the age of twenty-one, the young adult received something, such as money or livestock, to help give him or her a start in life.[1]

The government authorities of the time did not pay much attention to the way people treated their indentured servants. Their employers could treat them like members of the family—or like slaves. Only in cases of extreme abuse would a local magistrate decide that the contract between the employer and the indentured servant was void.[2] There was no general child protection law in the United States until the late 1800s. What changed things was the 1874 case of Mary Ellen, a nine-year-old indentured to Francis and Mary Connolly. The Connollys whipped her every day, stabbed her with scissors, and tied her to a bed. A church worker who intervened in the case had to rely on a law that protected animals from cruelty. The next year, New York State passed the nation's first law governing the protection of children.[3]

From Almshouses to Orphanages

Throughout the late 1700s and the early 1800s, many towns and cities supported almshouses, group living quarters that provided only the barest necessities for those unable to care for themselves. Many Americans of that era believed that the poor deserved nothing better, and that poor people, young or old, had only themselves to blame for their condition. The annual report of the New York Almshouse Commissioners of 1847 expressed it this way: ". . . in our highly favored country, where labor is so much demanded and so liberally rewarded and the means of subsistence so easily and cheaply obtained, poverty need not and ought not to exist."[4] The very young and the very old, as well as other adults, struggled to stay alive on their town's meager supplies in these institutions. Some communities continued to have almshouses, also known as poorhouses, through the end of the 1800s.

Americans who cared about the welfare of others saw that the almshouse was a poor environment for children. The select committee of a state senate, for instance, described almshouses in an 1856 report as poor nurseries, encouraging the young people in them to depend on public charity rather than to become self-supporting adults.[5] Private charitable groups began to establish orphanages, special institutions that would care only for children.[6]

By definition, an orphan is a child with no living parents. But even when orphanages were first founded in this country in the middle of the 1800s, most of them also accepted children whose parents were unable to care for them, as well as children whose parents had died. The private charities or church groups that founded 90 percent of the orphanages in the late 1800s were entirely dependent on charitable contributions. These could vary from year to year. If contributions dropped, the children went hungry.[7] After the Civil War, eight states opened orphanages to care for the children of soldiers who had been killed in that conflict.[8] Public or private, orphanages accepted children up to about age eight. They "graduated" long before they became adults, usually at about age twelve. Then they became indentured servants, working for their keep, until age eighteen or nineteen.[9]

Orphanages in the 1800s were almost always segregated by race. Most accepted only white children. Just a few were founded to care for African-American children. When these segregated orphanages were full, young African-Americans had nowhere else to go but to the almshouses.[10] Also, many orphanages were single sex; they accepted only boys or only girls. They aimed to create a highly regulated system, more like a strict boarding school than a family home. Orphanages stressed discipline. Some even included military drills several times a day.[11] The schedules were rigidly planned, and the ratio of children to staff was high. Orphanage life did not give children much chance to form close relationships with caring adults.

Free Foster Homes

New forms of care developed in the middle years of the 1800s that were meant to give homeless or neglected children a feel for family life. In New York and Chicago, two men started placement agencies that arranged for children to live in what were called *free foster homes*. The homes were free in the sense that the foster parents in the arrangements were not paid for caring for the children placed with them. Charles Loring Brace, and several other Protestant ministers, founded the New York Children's Aid Society in 1853, and Martin Van Arsdale founded the State Children's Home Society of Illinois in 1882. They were responding to the problem of *street arabs*, or "ragged boys." These children, neither in school nor working, roamed the streets of most large American cities.

Children in free foster homes were expected to work for the family in return for room and board just as indentured servants had done. The difference was that they were supposedly "free" to leave at any time.[12] Of course, for a child from New York City placed on a farm in Ohio, this freedom did not mean very much. Most of the children who were placed by the New York Children's Aid Society ended up a long way from their original homes. The society obtained legal guardianship of these children from their surviving parents or guardians. Groups of children then traveled out of the city, supervised by one of the society's agents. The society always referred to its *placings-out* as being in the West, but the direction was just as often south or north. Groups of children might be taken to upstate New York, to the Midwest, or even as far away as Florida or Texas, but it was always toward farm country. Reverend Brace and other founders of the society were great believers in fresh country air and hard physical work.[13]

Before leaving by train with his group of twenty or thirty children, the society's agent had chosen a likely town and had organized a committee of the town's business people, usually headed by the local pastor. This committee handled publicity for the coming event of the children's arrival, and screened the applicants who wanted to have children placed in their homes. When the agent and the children arrived, the committee took charge of the temporary housing and feeding of the children. Then the agent handed them over to the chosen applicants, who were most often farmers. The families promised to care for the children until they turned twenty-one. In return, the children provided labor on the farm.[14]

The only written agreement between the society and the family was a card given to the person accepting a child. By taking the card, he or she agreed to provide the child with a good education and proper care. For its part, the society agreed to remove the child if he or she proved unsatisfactory, or for any other justifiable reason, and to pay the child's fare back to New York City. The guardianship of the child remained with the society and was not transferred to the person taking the child, even though the society's agents might be hundreds of miles away in New York City. Society agents generally contacted each family with a placed-out child once a year for the first few years, then more irregularly.[15]

The New York Children's Aid Society and other urban agencies following the society's practices placed some 150,000 children outside the cities of the Northeast in the years 1853 to 1929.[16] These placement programs were always controversial. For one thing, the society was Protestant. Catholic religious leaders strongly objected to the children of Catholic parents being placed in Protestant homes. Eventually, the Catholics formed their own agency, the Protectory. The Protectory placed orphaned or neglected Catholic children in Catholic homes in other states.

Another problem was that some of the children, especially the older boys and girls, ran away from their placements. A small percentage of these runaways became homeless or got into trouble with the law. Local authorities complained that New York was attempting to get rid of its criminal juveniles by shipping them out of state. Eventually, midwestern state legislatures began to react against the practice of placing-out in free foster homes by societies outside the state. In the 1890s, Michigan, Indiana, Illinois, and Minnesota all passed laws limiting placing-out.[17]

The Foster Boarding Home

The foster boarding home of the kind that is most common today, in which foster parents receive money for caring for children, came into existence in the early 1900s. Charles Birtwell of the Boston Children's Aid Society was the first to pay foster parents for the keep of the children in their care. Parents in foster boarding homes who received money for the children's food and clothing, the theory went, would not need to have the children perform hard labor in return for their room and board. Birtwell hoped this would encourage foster parents to treat the children more like family members and less like hired servants.[18] He also developed the first systematic plans for evaluating the fitness of would-be foster parents and for supervising the care of children who had been placed with them.[19]

In 1909, President Theodore Roosevelt convened the White House Conference on the Care of Dependent Children. The conferees agreed that children should, if possible, remain in their own homes. Poverty alone should not be a reason to take children away from their biological parents. They also agreed that if foster care was needed, it was better offered in homes than in institutions like orphanages.[20] People who attended this conference pointed out, however, that up to that time there had been few investigations comparing children in institutions and those in foster care. Very few facts were available about the effects of the different kinds of care on children who were living away from their original homes.[21] Since then, many sociologists have studied the effects of foster care on children (see chapter 8, Leaving Foster Care).

When people use the term foster care today, they usually refer to a child's placement in a household that receives money from an agency to cover the costs of the child's basic needs. Over the course of this century, these foster boarding homes became the most popular kind of care for the homeless or maltreated child. In 1923, 64 percent of children receiving care were in residential institutions. By 1933, fewer than half the children in care, or 48 percent, were in institutional settings. By 1969, the number in institutional placements had fallen farther, to only 18 percent of children in care.[22] Some residential institutions still exist today, but they care for less than 10 percent of the children in placement. Many of today's institutions use a cottage system. In each cottage, a small group of children lives with a married couple, creating a homelike setting within the larger institution.

In the years after the White House Conference, the Children's Bureau of the United States Department of Labor encouraged states to start providing social services for children. They recommended using a social casework model. In this model, a trained representative of the child welfare agency works individually with a child and the child's family, providing counseling and practical help. Large private organizations such as the Boston and New York Children's Aid Societies sponsored child welfare work in most major cities in the early 1900s. In small towns and in the countryside, things were less organized. Still, twelve states had created county boards or departments to make social welfare services available to children by 1931.[23]

Federal Money for Foster Care

The federal government began to make money available to support child welfare when Congress passed the Social Security Act in 1935, during the economic hard times of the Great Depression. Unemployment was high, and many people were unable to provide for their children. The administration of President Franklin Roosevelt designed the Social Security Act to provide for the well-being of many struggling groups. These groups included "homeless, dependent, and neglected children, and children in danger of becoming delinquent."[24] By the end of 1939, every state had organized a child welfare program.[25]

The amount of money the federal government spent supporting child welfare work in 1936 was one and a half million dollars, a very small amount in comparison with what is spent today. According to one estimate, in 1990 the federal government spent a thousand times as much on foster care for children receiving welfare, or over one and a half *billion* dollars.[26] Costs were low at first because federal money supported foster programs only in rural areas during the first twenty years of federal involvement. Since 1958, federal money has supported foster care in cities as well as in the country.[27]

The system created in 1935 provides the model for the system of social services for children that exists today. In the case of foster care, federal money supports most foster care for children whose families are not financially able to provide for them. It also pays for some pilot projects. State and private organizations provide other programs, and state or city agencies often sign contracts with the private agencies to find placements for the foster children they have taken into care.

Today's Foster Care Policies

In the late 1930s, when foster care programs were first available nationwide, the emphasis was on caring for children away from their own homes, either in group homes or in private foster homes.[28] But in recent years, social welfare policy has moved away from the idea that helping children always, or even usually, means removing them from their original homes. Increasingly, planners have emphasized preserving and supporting the child's biological family. In programs of family preservation, social welfare departments provide help and support to the family in its own home. The idea is to make it possible for children to remain in their original homes and prevent the need for foster placement.

The other change in child welfare policy has been the move toward permanency planning. According to this policy, every child deserves a stable, supportive, permanent home. A child who drifts along in foster care lacks this basic security. Those who support permanency planning argue that when a child leaves his or her home, there should be a relatively quick decision about what will happen. Will the child ever be able to return home? If it seems likely that he or she will, then the social welfare system should provide the biological parents with strong support so that they can solve their problems and be reunited with their children. Or does it seem as though the family can never be reunited? If so, then the social welfare system should move to terminate parental rights so that the child is free to be adopted into a new family. Both these concepts received strong legal backing in the Adoption Assistance and Child Welfare Reform Act of 1980, PL 96–272. This act, which is discussed in more detail in chapter 7, continues to shape the operation of the foster care system in the United States today.

3 Why Children Enter Care

In 1991, 340,000 children in the United States were estimated to be in foster care.[1] When presented with this fact, the first question most of us ask is "Why?" Most Americans think of the normal family arrangement as one in which parents are raising their own children in the way they see fit.[2] Yet there are hundreds of thousands of cases in which parents lose the right to raise their children themselves, and other cases where they choose to give up that right. No two cases in which things go seriously wrong in a family are exactly alike, but there are some common areas in which the problems tend to occur.

Poor Children and Minority Children

One very important factor that affects which children will enter foster care is family income. It is true that children from well-to-do or middle-income families, as well as children from poor families, sometimes find themselves in foster homes. But the poorer the child's family, the more likely that the child will be placed in foster care. Statistics do not show clearly how many foster children come from poor families. Still, of those 360,000 or so in care in 1988, at least 123,000, or more than one in three of the estimated total, were from families with incomes low enough to qualify for help from the government under the Aid for Families with Dependent Children program.[3]

Race is another factor that, in combination with poverty, affects a child's likelihood of being placed in foster care. Parents who are members of minority groups are often poor. According to a House Select Committee Report on Children, Youth, and Families in 1989, minority children made up 46 percent of the foster care population in 1988.[4] A study in 1986 found that Native American children were being placed in foster care at a rate three times as great as non–Native American children.[5]

Why should child welfare agencies find it necessary to place poor and minority children in foster care more often than other children? Poor families with limited resources, especially if they are living in low-income neighborhoods or communities, may have little to draw upon if there is a family crisis. If a parent loses a job, or if the family loses its apartment, the family may break up. A single parent without an income or a place to live may be unable to care for the children. A richer family might be able to turn to other family members for help, but poor families without these resources see their children placed in foster care.[6] A 1987 study showed that 30 percent of African-American foster children in five major cities went into care from inadequate housing, and another 11 percent were homeless.[7] And the problem of homelessness has grown worse since then.

Other parents, poor or not, have emotional problems that lead them to maltreat their children or fail to provide them with what they need to develop into healthy, mature individuals. Placing children in care to protect them from abuse and neglect is common. This is, in fact, the reason for most placements of children under the age of six.[8] Nationwide, 54 percent of the children placed in foster care in 1986 were taken from their parents as a protective measure.[9]

Abuse and neglect is a broad category. It covers many kinds of maltreatment, from failing to provide children with food or clothing through battering them. Research on abusive and neglectful families has shown that there are, in general, four ways in which parents put their children in danger: physical neglect, physical abuse, sexual abuse, and emotional maltreatment.[10] Those who abuse their children in these ways sometimes have certain psychological problems in common.

Child neglect is the more common and widespread problem of the two, occurring twice as often as child abuse. Among abused and neglected children who are hurt badly enough to be hospitalized, two and a half times as many have been neglected as have been abused.[11] In more than 50 percent of these cases, neglect means that the parent left the child at home unattended.[12] The connection with poverty is clear. A parent who has little or no money may leave her child alone so that she can, for instance, do her chores or go to work. A parent who can afford it will hire a baby-sitter or will pay for day-care.

Alcohol and Drug Abuse

One group of parents at special risk for neglecting their children are those who abuse alcohol or drugs. For parents addicted to these substances, the risk is even higher. Alcoholism or drug addiction of a parent or parents, in itself, is not a reason for placement, although addicts often mistreat or neglect their children. In many of these cases, placement then becomes necessary. In New York State, a survey found that parental drug or alcohol abuse was a factor in more than 60 percent of foster placements.[13]

Crack cocaine abuse swelled into an epidemic in the late 1980s. Its victims ignored their children as well as much else around them while under the influence of this extremely addictive drug. Crack use not only contributes to the problem of neglect but also affects many of the babies born to addicted mothers. As a result of exposure to cocaine before birth, babies may not be very responsive to the people around them, and they are not easily made comfortable. The mother thus has a withdrawn, irritable infant to deal with, in addition to the problems of her own addiction. In many cases, she is also poor. These mothers are at special risk of neglecting their children.[14]

The problem of crack-addicted mothers was especially acute in the years between 1987 and 1990. In New York City, for instance, the number of children in foster care more than doubled, rising to 50,000 children in care.[15] State laws prohibiting group care for children younger than age five were temporarily relaxed during the height of the crack epidemic. Emergency group homes were opened to care for the large numbers of newborns and infants born to addicted mothers incapable of caring for them who had, in many cases, simply abandoned them.[16] Private social welfare agencies also made short-term foster placements of the newborns, until relatives or friends of the parents could be found to care for them.[17]

Children who are born to addicted or seriously ill parents—mothers with AIDS, for instance—in many cases are addicted or ill themselves. Sick or addicted children demand special care. As AIDS affects more young women, the problem grows larger. In 1990, more than 2,500 cases of AIDS were reported among infants in the United States, with over 700 in New York City alone.[18] Only one child in three who tests positive at birth for the HIV virus will actually develop AIDS. In two-thirds of the cases, the babies show antibodies transmitted by their mothers, but are not actually infected. Whether they themselves are infected or not, a majority of the children born to mothers who are HIV-positive are likely to need substitute care at some point during their childhood. If a single mother dies of AIDS, for instance, her children are orphaned.

Physical Abuse

Other parents abuse their children physically. Physical punishment of children is accepted as normal in some communities. Even in these communities, the parents who are defined as abusers step over any line of normality. They inflict psychological as well as physical damage on their children. Often, it is not the child's behavior that causes the child to suffer physical abuse. Instead, these abusive parents strike out at their children because of their own problems and frustrations. Such abuse is far from rare: some 575,000 cases of physical assault on children were reported in 1987. The same report indicates that between 2,000 and 5,000 children die every year as a result of physical abuse.[19] Reports of abuse continue to increase every year.

Children who are removed from their homes because they have suffered violent physical abuse have a particularly difficult time in recovering psychologically from their experiences. One study showed that boys who had been physically abused were at great risk of getting into trouble with the law in their early teens, doing badly in school, and becoming involved in crime, especially violent crime, as adults.[20] It is very important, both for them and for our society, that children who have been physically abused before they are placed in foster care get the opportunity to deal with the psychological effects of the abuse. Counseling or discussions with their social worker or their foster families may help abused children to work through their feelings about what happened to them, put the events behind them, and avoid long-term aftereffects.

32

War has always left orphans in its wake. This engraving, entitled The Soldier's Orphans, *dates from the American Civil War.*

Until the 1950s, the orphanage was the predominant institution for harboring children who had lost their parents. Typically, the orphanage was a cold, bleak place, and no substitute for a caring home. This photo was taken in 1889 of the Five Points House of Industry, an orphanage in New York City.

WANTED

YOUNG SKINNY WIRY FELLOWS not over eighteen. Must be expert riders willing to risk death daily. Orphans preferred. WAGES $25 per week. Apply, *Central Overland Express, Alta Bldg., Montgomery St.*

This 1860 newspaper advertisement for pony express riders states "orphans preferred," because the work was fraught with danger and orphans were considered expendable.

Rather than place children in orphanages in the late 1800s, child welfare workers sent city orphans to live with farm families who needed help on their farms. This arrangement was a forerunner of today's foster care system.

In the 19th century, abandoned children would often seek work in factories or mines to survive. The boys above were mine workers. The boys on the right were chimney sweeps.

"Street Arabs" was the name for children who lived in the streets. Often children of poor immigrant parents had no relatives in the United States who could take them in once their parents were gone.

Above: *Prostitution has often been the fate of abandoned children. This young girl in Thailand has come from the countryside to the city to be a prostitute.*

Facing page, bottom: *Homeless boys living together in the streets of Kathmandu, Nepal, in 1985.*

Facing page, top: *Street children sleeping in Rio de Janeiro, Brazil. The United Nations estimates that there may be more than 10 million abandoned children between seven and seventeen years old living in the streets of Brazil. Their families are so poor that the children must leave home to support themselves.*

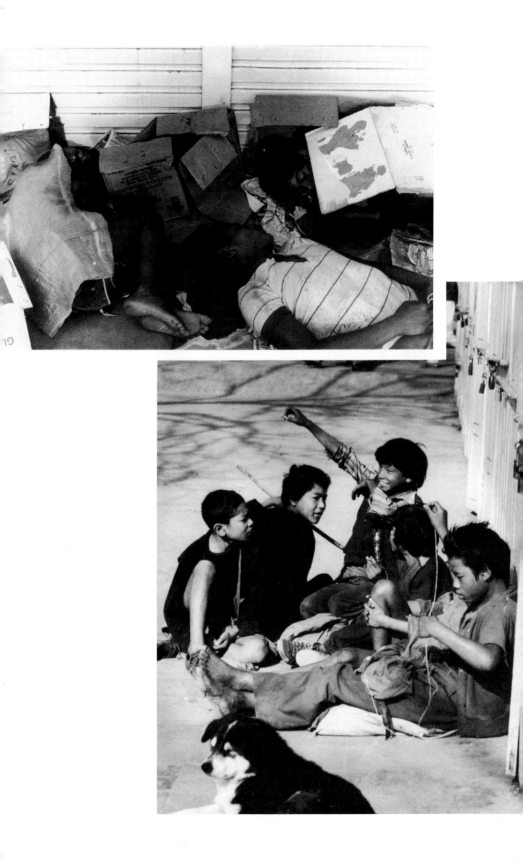

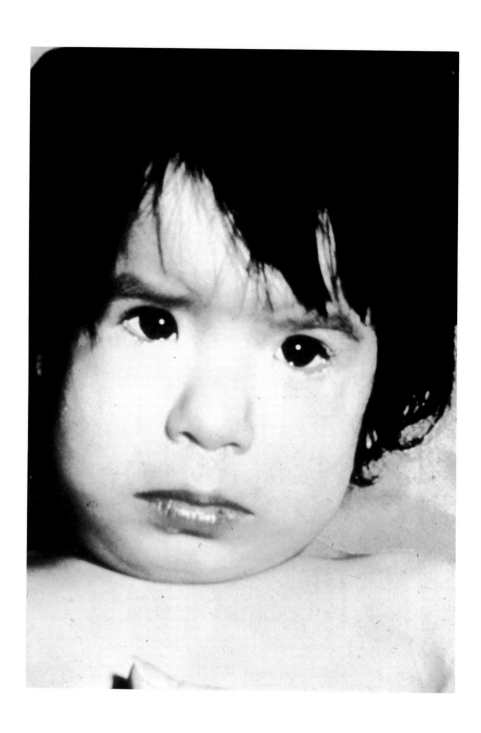

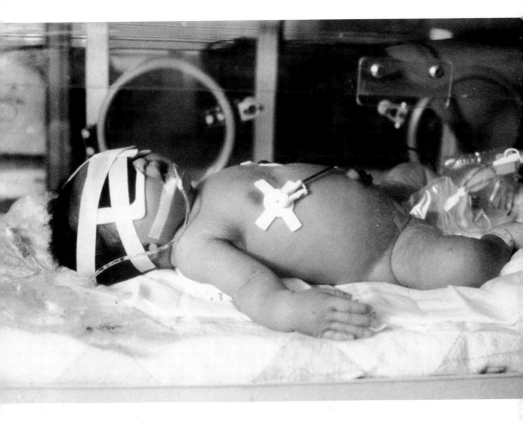

Above: *The crack epidemic has been responsible for an increase in the numbers of children overloading the foster care system because addicted parents are not capable of caring for children. In addition, babies born to mothers who smoked crack during pregnancy have many serious ailments and require long-term hospital care.*

Facing page: *Children need to live in a foster family for many different reasons. This toddler is afflicted with Fetal Alcohol Syndrome because his mother drank alcohol when she was pregnant. The mother is still an alcoholic and cannot take care of the baby.*

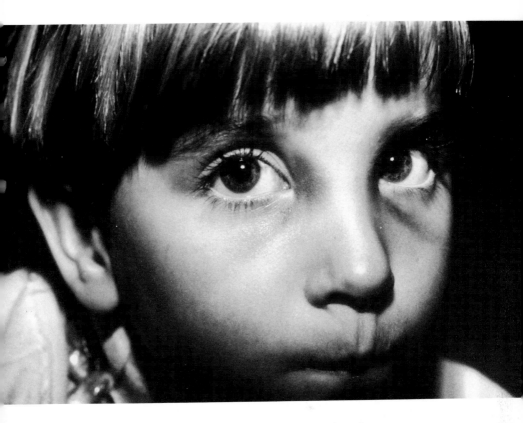

Above: *This young girl has fading marks of two black eyes. Battered children must be removed from abusive parents for their protection and placed in foster care. In recent years, the number of reports of physical and sexual abuse of children has doubled.*

Facing page: *This foster child is sick with AIDS, the disease that has already killed her mother. The infant contracted the HIV virus from the mother while still in the womb.*

Mother Clara Hale (shown here with two of her foster children) founded Hale House in New York City to give a home to abandoned babies born addicted to drugs or suffering from AIDS.

Children who have been removed from their families or who have been abused often suffer emotional pain. A good foster care system provides therapy for these children. This little boy is doing "play therapy" with a counselor.

Above: *Teenagers need a warm and caring foster family as much as younger children do. These two Amerasian teenagers (left) share photos with their foster parents (right).*

Facing page: *Today many grandmothers are taking care of their grandchildren when the parents are incapacitated. Caseworkers often attempt to place children with family members rather than with strangers. This is called kinship foster care.*

A caseworker at a child welfare agency talks with a client.

Sexual Abuse

Another type of abuse is sexual in nature. Some parents have serious psychological problems that lead them to have sexual relations with their children. Or others in the household, such as a stepparent or boyfriend, may make sexual advances to a child, with or without the knowledge of the biological parent. One report of child abuse nationwide showed that 14 percent was sexual in nature. About 50 percent of these cases involved either a biological parent or a stepparent.[21] In most cases, the victim of child sexual assault is female, and the abuser is an adult male.

Unlike neglect, sexual abuse is not a function of poverty. Its devastating effects may be found in every economic group. While sometimes there may be debate about whether a particular case of physical punishment does or does not represent maltreatment, there is no such debate in cases of sexual abuse. No community views sexual relations between adults and the children in their homes as normal.

There is, however, a problem with secrecy. Sexual abuse often does not leave visible scars. It is hidden, and it is likely to continue unless the victim speaks out. The social service community must rely on the victim, or a member of the victim's family, to come forward and disclose the abuse. The child then needs support to stand firm in the face of the family denials that may follow.[22] It is more common for the social service agency to bar the perpetrator of the abuse from the home than to remove the victim. However, in some cases, short-term foster placement is part of the treatment. Not only does placement prevent further abuse, it also relieves the child from any pressure to change his or her story that may come from members of the family if he or she remains in the home.

While abuse and neglect are the most common reasons for children being placed in foster care, there are others. One recent study showed that the condition of the parents accounted for 17 percent of the children placed in care.[23] If a single parent is hospitalized, placed in a mental institution, or sent to prison, children may stay with relatives or family friends. But if there are no willing substitute caregivers, the children must be placed in foster care. This situation is becoming more common as more women are sent to prison and as more young adults of both sexes, especially among the poor, become ill with AIDS.

How Abuse Affects Children

All these reasons for children entering care—neglect, physical abuse, sexual abuse, parents who are in hospitals or prisons—have a serious impact on the children. Neglected and abused children try to survive as best they can, and one way of surviving is by forgetting or holding back their powerful feelings about the terrible things that have happened to them. One way of forgetting is by cutting themselves off emotionally from the people responsible, the parents and parent-figures who neglected or abused them.

A child who is emotionally distant from members of his or her own family is unlikely to have sympathetic feelings for those outside the family. One study suggests that because neglected and abused children often have little human sympathy left, some of them may be more vulnerable to developing delinquent, violent, or criminal behavior than young people who were not neglected or abused. The study further shows that the more severely neglected or abused a child has been, the more likely the child will be to participate in violence against others.[24]

Behavior Problems

While younger children are most often placed in foster care because of parental abuse or neglect, older children tend to be placed because of their behavior. A *New York Times* story reported that 11 percent of the children entering care did so because of behavior problems.[25] A Congressional committee report in 1988 showed juvenile arrests for violent crime on the increase and noted that almost 1.2 million children run away from home each year.[26] Many of these young people are victims of abuse. In other cases, the parents of these children feel that they cannot handle them. The legal troubles of young people who become involved with the juvenile criminal justice system are often the so-called *status offenses*. This is a type of misbehavior such as being truant from school over and over or running away from home again and again that is specifically related to their status as dependent children.

But placement in such cases may not always be advisable. Authorities on child welfare argue that in most cases the best treatment of status offenses is social service for the family. Counseling can help children cope and can also support mothers and fathers in their efforts as parents. If it is possible, helping parents and children work out their difficulties is preferable to a court-ordered separation of the family members. In one case in Washington, for example, the child welfare system intervened in a family disagreement and represented a girl against her parents, breaking up the family as a result. Fifteen-year-old Cynthia's father brought her to a juvenile home because she was defying parental rules on smoking and dating. She asked to be placed in a foster home, and the child welfare agency placed her. Her parents sued the state for the return of her guardianship to them, but during the three years it took for the issue to be resolved in the courts, any chance for real family reconciliation was lost.[27]

Foster placements, as we have seen, may come about because of abuse, neglect, parental illness or imprisonment, or behavior problems so severe that parents throw up their hands. In many cases, more than one of these factors is involved. All of these indicate serious difficulties in family interaction, and all demand remedies. People who consider the issue of foster care tend to think of the common features of groups of cases, such as those of cocaine-addicted infants or of sexually abused adolescents. It is important to remember that these common features do not adequately explain the problems, or the potential, of the individuals involved in any single placement. Each case represents a separate, unique, and generally desperate human story. Each demands an individual answer.

4 Life in Foster Homes

The experience of being taken away to a foster home is traumatic for any child. Children show signs of emotional stress during the early weeks and months of placement. These may include nightmares, trouble in sleeping, bed-wetting, and eating problems.[1] Most such physical symptoms disappear after the first few weeks of placement, but the emotional problems continue.

Foster Children's Feelings

Children in care are often unhappy, even when the homes from which they have been removed were unpleasant or unsafe places for them to be. A household that looks bad to outsiders—where there is neglect or abuse, for instance—still represents normal life to the child who resides in it. The child of a home in crisis has strong attachments to his or her parent or parents, just as other children do. Children understandably feel insecure, depressed, and angry when removed from the way of life they know best.

Confusion and insecurity are especially likely if no one explains the situation to the child. Many children are never informed about why they are being placed in foster care. In one study, four of five foster children interviewed did not understand why they had been placed. In addition, some children who had been placed in foster homes because of conditions over which they had no control believed that there were things they had to improve before they could return to their homes. Because they were not fully informed, they felt that the breakup of their families was their fault.[2]

One study showed that over 60 percent of children in foster homes openly admit to feeling angry or unhappy about being taken away from their original homes.[3] Children in foster placements sometimes dream that their families will be miraculously different if they can only get back to them, just as children whose parents have divorced may fantasize about the possibility of their parents getting back together and remarrying. The different way of life in a foster home, even if it is in some ways more comfortable or less painful than life with their own parent or parents, can seem unnatural. It is not surprising that children who are given a chance to talk about their experiences in foster homes often express a great deal of anger.[4]

The experience of being in foster care creates confusion as well as anger. The foster child strongly feels the anger and sadness of being separated from his or her original parents. At the same time, he or she feels a sense of relief at being out of the atmosphere of crisis at home. About 10 percent of foster children in one study openly admitted a feeling of relief at being removed from homes in which they had been neglected or abused.[5] Even in cases where a child is not able to admit it openly, moving into another home seems to help. There is specific evidence that being in foster care can help maltreated children recover. One study of physically abused children who had been placed in care found that their problem behavior had improved, especially their emotional withdrawal from other people, and they were much better at managing their hostility. The same study showed that neglected children, who tend to behave immaturely, started catching up with other children their own age while in foster care. They also learned to manage their anger more successfully and to get along better with other children. Neglected children in the same study also showed improvement in their behavior while in foster care.[6]

Chances to talk about their feelings with someone who understands are very important to foster children. The feelings that foster children have about being away from their homes don't ever go away. If they are not brought out into the open and discussed, they can do psychological damage, no matter how good the foster home is. At one group session where foster children got together to talk about their experiences and share feelings about being in care, the most common feeling they expressed was their opposition to being in foster homes. Older children felt anger about missing their friends, while younger children were sad about not being with their parents. The children in these groups agreed that it was good to get together with other foster children because it helped them to realize that they were not alone in their experiences.[7]

Ideally, of course, the best people for a child to talk with about feelings are the foster parents. They are there in the child's life every day. Interacting with them can provide the child with a way to work through feelings about separation from parents. If foster parents have received thorough training, they may be able to help a child mourn his or her losses, develop a new, trusting relationship with an adult, and retain a sense of self-worth. This kind of emotional healing is the best possible outcome of a foster care placement.[8] Unfortunately, it does not happen in every case.

Placements That Don't Succeed

Placement in one particular foster home may not last long. Children in foster care often move from home to home during their time away from their biological parents. Placements don't work out, for one reason or another, in a high percentage of cases. When this happens, foster parents request removal of the child from their home. A recent study estimates that between 25 and 30 percent of children now in foster care have been in three or more placements.[9] The average number of placements is even higher for teenagers in care.[10]

Foster parents sometimes choose to end a placement for reasons that have little or nothing to do with the foster child. They are neither the biological parents nor the legal guardians of their foster child. This lack of a real, permanent connection naturally affects the way that many foster parents view their relationships with their foster children. Circumstances in their lives may change in ways that make it more difficult, or even impossible, for them to continue as foster parents. A parent who has been a homemaker may choose to get a job outside the home, or the family may decide upon a long-distance move. They may then request a new placement for the child. No matter what the reasons are, though, foster children may blame themselves when a placement comes to an end.

In other cases, placements end because the foster child is in some way too difficult for the foster parents to deal with. After all, most foster children have had difficult, deeply unsettling experiences in their recent pasts. Neglect and abuse do not tend to create outgoing, cooperative human beings. Experts report that the foster child who has been physically or sexually abused by his or her biological parents has an especially hard time adjusting to foster care. "Thse kids are a lot harder to handle because of the psychological damage they've suffered. They don't trust adults, so for the foster care relationship to get going is almost impossible,"[11] explained Diane Flannery, executive director of New York's Larkin Street Youth Center.

Sometimes the mistrust is all too justifiable. Unfor-

40

tunately, foster children may be abused in their foster homes. One researcher estimated that over 10 percent of children placed suffered such abuse, abuse that ranged from beatings to broken bones.[12] Another recent study found that 25 percent of individuals who were interviewed after leaving foster care at age eighteen recalled severe physical punishment in their foster homes. Also, 24 percent of the girls and 8 percent of the boys in this study had experienced "a disturbing sexual event" in at least one of their foster placements.[13] The New York Times reported that, in 1990, three New York children taken from their homes had died in foster care.[14] The panel of experts who investigated these cases noted that all three were in the care of first-time foster mothers. The experts recommended greater care in the selection and training of foster parents.[15]

But even placements with carefully selected, well-trained, kind, and mature foster parents can fail. In part, because they are so mistrustful, foster children may respond to their arrival in a particular foster home by testing the placement. A child who has been in a foster home for a few weeks or months misbehaves in various ways. This acting out, psychologists say, is a way to see if the foster parents really care for them. Will the foster parents discuss the reasons for the misbehavior? Will they set appropriate limits? Unfortunately, what often happens is that the foster parents "fail the test." They find the child's misbehavior trying enough to request that the child be removed from their home. Testing the placement can become a pattern, with the child even more likely to misbehave in the next foster home. He or she may continue from placement to placement, suffering fresh psychological damage with every move.[16]

Placements fail for many reasons. In fact, there is little agreement about what factors make for a successful placement. One large research project concluded that success is "largely a matter of chance."[17] Multiple placements are common. Two studies in Canada, made twelve years apart, showed that on average children who were still in foster care when they became adults had lived in four different homes by that time.[18] A young Californian, Dennis Smith, sued the county in which he lived because he had lived in sixteen different foster homes by the time he was seventeen.[19]

When things don't work out in a foster home, the child naturally experiences feelings of failure. Dennis Smith put it this way: "It's like a scar on your brain; every time something bad happens, you wonder if you're going to another home."[20] As the number of placements goes up, it becomes harder and harder for a child to develop trust toward adults in general, and parental figures in particular. The more changes in residence a child has experienced, the more likely he or she is to be hostile and negative on a move into yet another setting.[21]

Those foster children who have experienced several placements understandably tend to have feelings of confusion about who they really are. All of us form our ideas about our identity partly in terms of other people—whose son or daughter or sister or brother we are. Young people who have always had one set of parents find it difficult to imagine trying again and again to adapt to different parent figures. Yet this is what foster children who experience more than one placement are called on to do. At the same time, they still retain their emotional ties to their biological parents. In many cases they love their biological parents very much. At the same time, their parents have hurt or disappointed them deeply. There may be others, too—biological and foster siblings, for instance—to whom they feel emotional loyalties. Some of these relationships with important people in a child's life may be over forever. In addition, foster children may well have had several caseworkers. Or they may have been in the care of more than one child welfare agency. Dealing with all these relationships, and all the losses, takes its toll on the foster child's sense of self-confidence and self-worth.[22]

Connections with Original Families

Foster children need a great deal of interpersonal support. The help their caseworkers provide is not enough. In fact, caseworkers themselves are increasingly aware of the importance of social support for a child going into a new foster home. Current thinking accepts the idea that it is best for children to maintain an ongoing connection with their original families. Naturally, this depends on the circumstances. Biological parents and foster parents need to be in touch with each other. Children benefit from regularly planned visits with their biological parents.[23] If the visits do not happen regularly, they can be stressful for the children.

Psychologists agree that the most intense loss a child can undergo is the loss of a parent. Continuing contact with biological parents is valuable for children even if the children and the parents are in conflict, according to the latest study by Daniel Fanshel. Professor Fanshel has done several large-scale investigations of foster care. He has learned that staying in touch allows the child to maintain a realistic view of the parent, which is not possible if the parent is absent from the child's life. On the basis of interviews with hundreds of former foster children, Dr. Fanshel concludes that a child in foster care is better off having to deal with a bad parent than wondering about an absent parent. His studies all show that foster children will be better off emotionally, unless there has been very serious physical abuse, if they continue to see their original parents.[24]

All too often, though, parents don't visit. In a two-year California study of five- to ten-year-olds in foster care, child welfare agencies allowed biological parents to visit their children once every week or two. There were thirteen children in the study. All of them wanted more visits from their parents when they were first placed in care. Twelve of the thirteen still wanted more visits after they had been in care for two years. When the children had been in care for just a few months, the majority of parents visited them regularly. However, after one year, only about one parent in three was still visiting every week or two. After three years, only one of the children's parents was still visiting every two weeks. Two parents of the thirteen never visited their children at all during their time in care.[25]

Feeling Different

Even in those cases where placements are working out, foster children frequently feel different from other children because they are not living with their own parents. Because they are very anxious not to be treated differently, some foster children experience difficulty in admitting to their friends, teachers, or others outside the home that they are in foster care. Almost 63 percent of a group of former foster children who were interviewed about their experiences admitted that they felt different, or set apart, from others of their age, and 58 percent said there were times when they did not want others to know they were in care.[26]

In their interviews, the former foster children recalled the day-to-day occurrences that reminded them of their status. Some remembered not having enough money to buy what their friends could. Others had been teased or ridiculed by their classmates for having a different name from their foster parents. Still others had been upset to find that other people had negative stereotypes about what foster children were like and assumed that they would behave badly. Another factor that separated them from other children was their agency contacts. They received regular visits from the caseworker at home or at school. They saw the agency doctor rather than going to their foster family's doctor. One former foster child summed it up this way, "You don't feel like an average kid."[27] Another added, "There should be a campaign that publicizes that foster children are people too."[28]

5

Foster Parents

In more than a hundred thousand homes all over this country, adults choose to take in and care for other people's children. Those who choose to do this demanding, uncertain work are the nation's foster parents. Caring for other people's children in one's own home is similar, in many ways, to caring for one's own children. As any parent knows, children require almost unlimited quantities of attention, time, and energy from their caregivers. Foster children often present a greater challenge to the adults with whom they live than do other children. Most of them have gone through recent difficult experiences, and they are facing the issue of separation from their biological parents. Foster parents have a major impact on the health, emotions, and development of their foster children during their time in care.[1] More than any other single element, they determine whether a placement will succeed or fail.

Why Take Foster Children?

Those who decide to take on the responsibility of caring for others' children have a variety of reasons for doing so. Some see the work as critically important for the children and for society as a whole. One woman who had cared for a total of fifty-five foster children put it this way: "These kids need to be in families rather than institutions. When they're in institutions, they don't know what it's like to live in a family, and they learn to be robots, often very destructive robots."[2] Another experienced foster parent said, "I thought I could save the world by becoming a foster parent. I now know that is impossible, but feel if we can give these children some safe, happy times, then we're doing our job."[3]

Another motivation for taking in foster children is the allowance or payment foster parents receive each month. Foster parents who welcome the money may also have a strong desire to do the important work of providing substitute care. But the income is important because most foster families are far from wealthy. In fact, some people accept several children and make foster parenting their full-time job.[4] Single women make up a significant percentage of foster parents today. Researchers in Connecticut found that single mothers headed 33 percent of the foster families in that state. Of these women, 47 percent (that is, about 15 percent of all foster parents) had incomes below the poverty level.[5] Supplemental income payments from the child welfare agency make a significant contribution to family income. Still, the checks from the agency must cover the expenses of the foster child's food and clothing, as well as other needs. In the Connecticut study, foster parents of adolescents were having an especially difficult time in meeting their children's material needs.[6]

The Foster Parent's Work

The job of foster parenting has various requirements. Some of these must be met even before a foster child is assigned to a home. First, foster parents must be licensed by the social service agency considering placing a child or children with them. An agency representative must inspect the would-be foster parents' home for health and safety features before the license is issued. In most states, those who will become foster parents are also required to attend training sessions before children are placed in their homes. At these sessions, workers or supervisors from the child welfare agency present information about the legal and practical responsibilities of foster parenting. They also suggest ways to handle typical problems.

Once the child is placed, the foster parent or parents take on the same responsibilities for that child's day-to-day activities that any parent has.[7] These responsibilities include seeing that the child gets regular meals, attends school, and gets to appointments with the doctor or therapist. Foster parents communicate regularly with the child's caseworker. They may also need to attend meetings with the child's teacher, or with any therapists who are treating the child. When the child needs items like clothes or school supplies, the foster parent or parents are expected to provide them.

A foster parent provides much more than just food, clothes, and transportation. He or she also takes on the difficult task of giving the child an ongoing, positive experience of life in a family. Everyone needs the ability to form close relationships with fellow human beings. We learn to do this within the family. Often, children placed in foster care have had bad experiences with the human connections in their birth families. The foster parent attempts to allow the child to connect to a different and healthier family unit and to experience a sense of continuity.[8]

In fact, this is the major reason child welfare reformers developed foster parenting. The reformers wanted to give maltreated children an opportunity to have good relationships with parental figures, and positive experiences of family life they were not getting in orphanages and other institutions. The intent was to protect children who could not live with their own parents from suffering long-term psychological damage as a result.

The Foster Parent Relationship

From the first days of the foster care system, it has been clear that the role of the foster parent is fundamentally different from the role of the biological parent. A foster parent's relationship with a foster child is closely, clearly, and precisely defined by law. In fact, before children come to the foster home, foster parents have signed a contract that spells out their responsibilities to the children, perhaps even down to the amount of pocket money they will dole out.[9] Unlike biological parents, they do not have the official legal responsibility, or guardianship, of the foster child or children. Whether they care for a child for a few weeks or for years, the guardianship of that child remains with the social welfare agency. The awareness that a social worker may appear at any time to take the child back to the biological parents certainly affects the relationship between the foster parent and the foster child.[10] In fact, some agencies actively discourage foster parents from forming an emotional bond with the children placed in their care.[11] Yet if an emotional bond does not form, the foster care relationship cannot give the child the psychological benefits it was developed to provide.[12]

The foster parent's relationship to the foster child is not as clear-cut as the words *parent* and *child* make it sound. Foster parents also interact regularly with a representative or representatives of the child welfare agency, most often the child's caseworker. Child welfare agencies are not in agreement as to how to view the foster family. Should the agency regard the foster parents as paid employees? As clients? As colleagues? Increasingly, as more children who have been severely abused enter foster care, the agencies are coming to regard the foster parents as a treatment resource. That is, ideally the foster parents can cooperate with the caseworker to help the child recover from the effects of the crisis that led to the foster placement.[13]

Interaction with Biological Parents

Depending on the social welfare agency's plan for the child, the foster parents may interact with the child's biological parents. In some cases, such as those where biological parents regularly visit their child, there may be frequent contact. These interactions may be disturbing, especially during the first days or weeks after a child has been placed, when the biological parents often find the placement difficult to accept. To get their children back, they must make changes in their lives, and many parents naturally resent having the need to change forced on them. This is particularly true if their problems are related to drug or alcohol abuse. They are likely to feel angry about their child's placement in a foster family. Many parents lose no time in communicating their anger to the foster parent or parents, as well as to the caseworker.[14]

If it is possible for the foster parents and the biological parents to overcome these strong negative feelings and maintain contact, they can both benefit. The child stands to benefit even more. If the biological parents stay in touch, they can give the foster parents information about their children's normal behavior, habits, and reactions to being disciplined, as well as information about the family's way of living. Foster parents can use this information to see that differences between the child's former and present lives do not seem too jarring. If the foster parents learn that there are major differences in the way things are done in the two homes, they will be able to encourage the children to talk about the differences. Children can have more continuity in their lives if communication is encouraged between their original and their foster homes.[15]

However, in one study where the child welfare

agency's policy officially stated that the foster parents and the biological parents should have a working relationship, only four of thirteen pairs of families interviewed knew each other. If the agency does not actively encourage such contact, it probably will not happen.[16] Of course, if certain types of physical or sexual abuse have occurred and seem likely to happen again, the agency must forbid contact until the parents can demonstrate that they have changed their behavior. In cases where there has not been abuse, it seems clear that contact would benefit both the families and the child.

Not an Easy Task

Obviously, being a good foster parent is a demanding and complex job. Perhaps because it is so difficult and does not pay particularly well, the number of foster families nationwide is declining. There were 147,000 foster families nationwide in 1987.[17] By 1991, this number had fallen to 125,000.[18] But the demand for foster homes had increased during the same period. The average number of children in each home had increased to three, double what it had been in 1980.[19] According to Gordon Evans, the director of the National Foster Parents Association, family economics is behind this drop in numbers. Many foster parents have found the money they get for foster care inadequate to support the children placed in their homes. Others, particularly the foster mothers who once stayed at home with their families, have found it necessary to take jobs outside the home in order to make ends meet.[20]

The National Commission on Family Foster Care recently reported another factor that accounts for the shrinking number of foster parents—their job is getting harder. Today's foster children are more troubled than those of ten or twenty years ago. The group's report on a year-long study noted that foster parents today "must respond to the developmental needs of youngsters who have been traumatized by poverty and homelessness, emotional maltreatment, physical and sexual abuse, alcohol and other drug exposure, [and] HIV infection. . . ."[21]

Guiding these traumatized children toward healthier development is not easy, but it is vital for our society that some adults be willing to make the effort. Being a foster parent requires an emotional commitment to a child that is powerful enough to allow that child to develop his or her human capacity for connection with others. The foster parent must combine this strong commitment with the ability to let go. The relationship of foster parent and foster child differs from other relationships because, from the moment it begins, the foster parents are working toward the goal of having the foster child leave their home and the system, and live in a permanent home. One manual for foster parent training put it this way: "Foster parents are not selected because they have chosen to make a lifetime commitment to a child, but rather because they have chosen to make a commitment to be meaningful during a child's lifetime."[22]

6   Caseworkers

Most foster care cases involve four parties, that is, people or groups of people: the child, the biological parent or parents, the foster parent or parents, and the child welfare agency. For the first three of these parties—the child, the biological parent, and the foster parent—a social worker or workers represent the child welfare agency. Several different caseworkers in the agency may be involved with a single case. Agencies have workers who specialize in finding foster homes and others who talk to children as they first enter care. The child's original family may have its own caseworker, a different person than the worker assigned to the child and the foster family. If the child has brothers or sisters in the system, they too may each have their own caseworker. Each of these individuals has a different perspective on the case.

These different viewpoints often create conflicts among the foster child, the child's original and foster parents, and the agency. In addition to the intense emotions that family issues bring out, foster care brings all the people involved face to face with the requirements of the legal system. It is the social worker, or caseworker, who must deal with the conflicts and problems that follow the placement of a child in foster care. The caseworker's job is to get involved with all the parties in the foster care system. He or she attempts to resolve conflicts, comply with legal requirements, and find solutions for the problem or problems that led to the placement.

The caseworker is on the front line of the efforts to work out the problems that placed the child in crisis, or is at least responsible for protecting the child from further damage while in the agency's care.

Caseworkers are a special breed. They are called upon to be fair, sympathetic, determined, diplomatic, and resourceful, and they must be excellent judges of character. In the eyes of the child, the child's parents, and the foster parents, the caseworker stands for the agency and, in a more general way, for the entire social service and legal system. By placing a family's child in foster care, the child welfare system has made a powerful statement to that family that changes are required. The caseworker is a key player in figuring out what these changes are and how the family can make them. He or she plays a critical role in determining what happens, or does not happen, in the lives of the troubled families of foster children.

The Case Plan

The law requires that a child welfare agency make a case plan for each child placed in foster care. The biological parents and the agency are expected to work out the plan cooperatively. In practice, however, it is usually developed by the caseworker and then signed by the child's parent or parents.[1] The social worker relies on this case plan as a guide for work with each individual child and family.

The plan covers three areas. First, it explains why the child has been placed in foster care. Second, it gives an estimate of the period of time the child will need to remain in care. Third, it spells out what conditions the biological parents must meet in order to demonstrate to the agency, and the court which ordered the placement, that they are ready to get back—and keep—the custody of their children.[2] One major responsibility of the social

54

worker is to take steps that will help put this plan into action.

Keeping Records Straight

Carrying out a case plan means providing support to all the groups involved in a particular foster care case. This involves talking and counseling, but it also means making practical arrangements. Social workers arrange for children in care to get any special professional help they need, such as appointments with a psychologist or sessions with a speech therapist. They arrange visits between biological parents and their children in care, perhaps picking up the child at the foster home and driving him or her to the visiting place and back.[3]

Bureaucratic tasks also consume a portion of every social worker's day. In one study, thirteen of fourteen caseworkers interviewed said that the demands of the child welfare bureaucracy, such as paperwork, problems with supervisors, and policy changes, were their biggest work problem. The same group of caseworkers spent an average of two hours of each workday on paperwork.[4]

The law requires child welfare agencies to maintain documentation of all the work they do. Caseworkers keep most of these records. For the agency, they fill out the necessary forms and legal documents that keep children's records up to date and show progress, or the lack of it, toward the plan's goals. Social workers also act for their agency in the courts. It is the social worker who presents information to the court when the child's case is up for review or when it is time to make a decision about the child's return to the biological parents.[5]

Communication Problems

The social worker needs to make sure that the child's biological parents understand the case plan and any changes made in it. If a foster child is ever going to return home to live with his or her biological parents again, it is critical that the parents fully understand this plan, since it explains what steps they must take before the family can be reunited. Yet not all social workers communicate this information effectively. One researcher interviewed biological parents about the changes that their case plans called on them to make. The social worker and the parents were more or less in agreement about what the parents had to do to get their children back in only five of thirteen cases.[6] In another study, 35 percent of parents did not understand what they had to do to get their families back together.[7]

Problems frequently arise in the relationships between caseworkers and the biological parents of children in foster care. The caseworkers, after all, must play two different roles with the parents, and these roles are often in conflict with each other. On the one hand, they are meant to be helpers and counselors, working to reunite parents and their children. At the same time, they are the representatives of the child welfare bureaucracy, and their jobs demand that they play by agency rules.[8] Many caseworkers understandably see the child and the child's well-being within the foster placement as their main responsibility. This sometimes leads them to view the biological parents as outsiders.[9]

Not surprisingly, the biological parents of children in care who are interviewed about their caseworkers are often highly critical of their performance. In one study, 25 percent of parents whose children had been placed did not understand why their children were in foster care. Of those whose children had been placed without a court decision—that is, with the parent's consent—38 percent said that they had been against the placements.[10] Clear channels of communication, perhaps the most important responsibility of the caseworker, are obviously lacking in some cases.

Caseloads

One factor that plays a major role in determining how successful a job caseworkers will be able to do is the size of their caseloads. In 1985, caseworkers in the special emergency response units that acted on reports of child abuse in California had an average caseload of almost thirty-three families.[11] The 1990 rate in New York City was not much better, with the typical caseworker assigned up to twenty-five families at a time.[12] In 1992, *Newsweek* noted that typical caseloads nationwide ranged from twelve to as many as ninety families.[13] And when Washington, D.C., was ordered to hand its child welfare system over to a private agency for necessary reforms, some of its caseworkers were handling up to 200 cases at a time.[14] Workers who are assigned the responsibility for such large numbers find that they must devote most of their effort to working with the foster children. They have little time or energy left to give to the biological parents. Yet the biological parents are as much in need of services as the children are if they are ever going to be reunited as families.[15]

Not all caseworkers face such heavy loads. Workers for a private child placement agency, Casey Family Services, are assigned only twelve to fifteen children at a time. Researchers studying Casey's success over a period of years saw this more reasonable caseload as one of the three special advantages of Casey Family Services.[16] According to the 1990 study, the agency helped children who had experienced multiple placements develop successfully into functioning adults. However, Casey Family Services draws upon funds endowed to the agency by its founder, United Parcel Service executive Jim Casey.[17]

The city and state child welfare organizations that handle most foster placements depend on allotments from governments that are increasingly hard pressed for funds. As the foster child population grows and public funds are cut, caseloads in these agencies become larger.

Training and Experience

Another important factor in caseworkers' success is their level of education and the amount of experience they have had in working with clients. In today's child welfare agency, these levels are often not very high. Only a minority of social workers have graduate degrees in their field. That is, they may have gone to college, but they have not studied social work policy questions in great depth. Caseworkers who have done additional college study specifically in the field of social work, and who have masters' degrees or higher, usually get a promotion. They move into positions in which they supervise other agency employees rather than working directly with parents and children.[18]

Perhaps the most difficult task the caseworker faces is finding the right way to be involved with a client sympathetically but objectively. Maintaining a professional distance helps the caseworker develop a realistic perspective on the client's problems and possibilities.[19] Finding the balance between sympathy and objectivity is especially difficult for caseworkers with limited experience. They tend either to think that their clients are completely unique, with problems that fit no recognized pattern, or to make grand generalizations that don't take the special features of each case into account.[20]

Surprisingly, not everyone agrees that experienced caseworkers do the best job. One major study of a large group of children who had been in foster care showed that inexperienced social welfare workers had a good effect on the children.[21] Foster children whose caseworkers had been on the job for less than three years tended to be more highly motivated, responsible, and sociable. The author of the study believes that the younger, less experienced caseworkers interest the children intellectually.[22] These young caseworkers just out of college may bring a fresh viewpoint to child welfare work. Some of the older and more experienced workers, on the other hand, may no longer find their work as interesting to them as it was at first. The children in their care may pick up on this lack of enthusiasm.

Whether caseworkers are new to the profession or not, they often do not stay with one assignment for long. Foster children frequently find that their caseworker has moved to another assignment or another agency, or that he or she has left social work altogether. A former foster child who had experienced frequent changes of caseworkers explained the effect on her this way: "Once I was finally able to trust one they were transferred, and then I would have to start all over again."[23] This is especially likely to be true of the young, just-out-of-college caseworker who may be using child welfare work as a transition to another career or to further study. Turnover is so great that a caseworker who has spent two years in a position is considered unusually experienced.[24]

How Children See Caseworkers

According to one recent study, caseworkers do succeed in forming generally positive relationships with the children assigned to them, although these relationships are not without problems. Of the 585 children interviewed, 90 percent felt that their caseworkers cared about them, and 87 percent said that the workers visited regularly and kept in touch. Also, 83 percent found the caseworker easy to talk with, and 70 percent said that they found the caseworker to be someone they could turn to when they had problems.[25] However, the same study suggests that there can also be significant gaps in communication between caseworkers and their charges. More than half the children complained that their caseworkers did not give them enough information about their biological families. Nearly half said that their caseworkers did not talk with them about how long they would stay in foster care, and almost 70 percent said they did not have discussions about the facts of life with their caseworkers.[26] Another study confirms this finding. In it, only about one former foster child in ten felt that he or she had been given enough information about sex and family planning, although one in four thought that this information should have been given a high priority.[27]

Obviously, there is plenty of room for improvement in the relationships of caseworkers and the foster children to whom they are assigned. Striving for improvement is worth it. When it works, a good relationship with a caseworker and the worker's agency can give a foster child a much-needed sense of connection and continuity. One man who had been in care with Casey Family Services for over five years had been lucky. He recalled, "I knew my photo was in their offices and I had a caseworker (the same one, not different ones like when I was under the state foster care system). Casey did a lot for me but this simple fact, that I belonged, was the most healing. It may not sound like much, but when one grows up in a world of continual crisis and disorganization, it means everything."[28]

7   **Foster Care Laws**

The idea that adults are legally responsible for children is so widely accepted in our society that most people never stop to think about it. Children up to the age of eighteen need not depend on themselves for life's essentials. Instead, they have the legal right to be supported by adults.[1] The law expects that adults will provide the children for whom they are responsible with the necessities of life: clothes, food, and shelter. Adults are also the ones responsible for children's receiving education and preparing for adulthood, and there is some expectation that they will control children's behavior. If a child does not attend school, for instance, or if he or she throws a rock through a neighbor's window, the responsible adult may end up in court. For most children, the responsible adults are their biological parents.

Legal Responsibility for Children

However, some parents are unable to do the job of parenting. Foster care law begins at the point where, for whatever reason, biological parents cannot be legally responsible for their children. At that point, the family court orders the child into foster care and legal guardianship of the child rests with the state rather than the parents. The court decides to do this if it finds that the circumstances in which the child is living are inappropriate, dangerous and against the law, and if the parents are unable or unwilling to change these circumstances. The court expects that guardianship will return to the parents as soon as conditions change. In the meantime, the judge generally awards the guardianship of the child to a child welfare agency.[2]

Children may be placed in care with or without their parents' agreement. Most often, parents do give their consent. For example, parents have agreed to placement in about two-thirds of cases, over the years, in New York City.[3] Whether the parents agree to have their child or children placed in foster care, or do not consent, the family court actually makes a decision about the case. Usually, a child welfare agency will file a petition of neglect, abandonment, or abuse; the court will then respond to it.[4] All states have laws that give courts the power to decide if a child has been maltreated and then take appropriate action.[5] Child welfare legislation in each state spells out the circumstances under which child welfare agencies may petition the court to allow the child to be placed in care.

When the State Can Intervene

While these circumstances vary somewhat from state to state, the reasons for children being placed in the care of an agency tend to fall into three categories. The first is neglect: a parent or parents are judged incapable of providing a child with the basic necessities for life. Often this is because the parents themselves are physically or mentally ill, or because they misuse alcohol or other drugs. The second is abuse: child welfare authorities learn that a parent or parents have physically, emotionally, or sexually harmed the child or have knowingly allowed other adults to do so. The third is incorrigibility: behavior by the child that parents find themselves unable to control or correct.

In most states it is possible to remove a child from

the home for a brief period of time in an emergency, even before the family court hears the case. A child who clearly shows marks of physical abuse, for instance, may be kept from returning to the home where the abuse occurred while the necessary legal arrangements are made. Once a child's custody has been transferred to the child welfare agency, the agency becomes the child's substitute parent.[6] Custody returns to the parents only when the court decides that the parents have met the conditions it set forth.

A great many legal issues surround the separation of children from their biological parents. Courts decide whether or not to remove a child from the home. They also establish exactly what the parents must do to get the child returned to them, and what contact will be allowed between parents and children while they are separated. After the child has been placed in a foster home, courts become involved in determining if the parent or parents have done what is necessary for the family to be reunited. Eventually, courts determine what will happen if the parent continues to be unable or unwilling to resume legal responsibility for the child.

Perhaps the most controversial questions that come up in family court center on the termination of parental rights. When, if ever, should parents' rights to be responsible for their own children be ended and given to other adults? To put it another way, when should another adult be able to adopt a child who has a living parent or parents?

An Important Federal Law

A federal law passed in 1980 has had a major effect ever since it was enacted. It not only affects whether children enter foster care, but it also shapes the ways in which agencies deal with the children in their custody. This law is the Adoption Assistance and Child Welfare Act, PL

96–272. It requires states to make reasonable efforts at keeping troubled families together in their own homes before removing children to foster care. The law emphasizes social services intended to help troubled families stay together, that is, it tries to keep children out of foster care. Families get these services in their own homes, and they may include counseling for the family, day care, housing assistance, or homemaking help.[7]

The act also sets a limit of eighteen months as the period of time within which the court must make a decision about a child's permanent placement and a plan to carry it out—in exceptional cases it extends to two years. One family policy expert has compared this setting of a limit to the provisional decree of divorce given in many states at some fixed date before the divorce becomes final.[8] Divorce law sets a point in time at which a couple must officially recognize that the structure of their marriage has greatly changed. At that point, they must either decide to end their marriage legally, going forward to a final decree of divorce, or must reconcile and end the divorce proceeding. The limit of eighteen months to two years set by PL 96–272 recognizes that the chances of a child's returning home decline dramatically after the child has spent two years in foster care.[9] The intent of the limit is to prevent the child from drifting on and on in what is supposedly a temporary arrangement, and to move the child toward a secure permanent home. In some cases, this limit gives agencies the go-ahead to press for termination of parental rights so that a child is freed for adoption. Another new limit in PL 96–272 is that it sets six months as the maximum period of time over which parents may voluntarily put their children into foster care.[10]

In addition, PL 96–272 has several requirements intended to create a clear record of children's progress through the system. Clear records are important in making the handling of foster care placements more systematic and uniform from one agency to another. Under PL 96–272, agencies are required to keep a record of what preventive services were offered to a child's family before the child's placement in foster care. They must maintain an inventory of children in care, and they are required to use an effective tracking system for children in care so that there is a dependable record of each child's placement history.[11]

According to PL 96–272, each child is to have a case plan made for his or her individual situation. Within sixty days of the time a child enters agency custody, the agency must write a plan for that child's care which includes the eventual goal of the placement. The law emphasizes permanency planning, or the idea that children deserve to remain in one stable setting. There are two possible permanent residences for children: with their biological parents or with adoptive parents. (By definition, foster care is not permanent.) Either a return home or an adoption is usually the stated goal of a case plan. The court, or a citizen review committee in the community, approves the plan, and after that, the child's case comes up for review by the court every six months. At these reviews, the social welfare agency presents an update of any progress toward the goals of the case plan, as well as any changes in the goals.[12]

Each state's child welfare agency receives a share of the $1.5 billion a year that the federal government allocates for foster care under the Aid to Families with Dependent Children program (AFDC). If a state does not provide the services required by PL 96–272 that attempt to keep children in their own homes and out of foster placement, the federal government may withhold part of the state's foster care funds. But, according to a Supreme Court decision of March 1992, only the federal government may force changes in this way. The Court reversed a lower court's decision in a lawsuit on behalf of children in the foster care system in Illinois. The lawsuit had attempted to force the state to appoint a caseworker within three days for each child taken into custody by the state's child welfare service. The Supreme Court decided that private civil rights lawsuits could not be brought against states to try to force them to provide such services.[13]

Permanency Planning

PL 96–272 made permanency planning a national goal for the child welfare system. Permanency planning, an idea that developed in the 1970s, was a response to the large numbers of children who appeared to be drifting along for years in foster care with little thought being taken for their future. What PL 96–272 supports is either returning children to their own homes or freeing them for adoption. The law provides funds to make a plan for permanency for each child. It includes a list of the possible permanent plans in the order lawmakers considered best to worst. Prevention of out-of-home placement is at the top of the list, and long-term foster care is at the bottom.[14]

At least during its initial years, PL 96–272 seemed to be doing what it was written to do. The number of children nationwide in out-of-home placements dropped from 502,000 in 1977 to 243,000 in 1982. During the same years, the average time each child spent in care dropped from forty-seven to thirty-five months. However, critics of PL 96–272 have suggested that the system is still not doing a good job for the neediest children. Numbers in care nationwide began to rise again in the mid-1980s, reaching 360,000 by 1987 and continuing to rise today.[15] Some experts predict that up to a million children will be living apart from their families by the end of the 1990s.[16] While younger children may indeed be leaving the system more quickly, older children as well as minority children and those with special needs all too often still drift from placement to placement over a period of years.[17]

State Laws and Courts

The specifics of child welfare policy are spelled out at the state level rather than the national level. There are fifty different, although loosely related, bodies of child welfare law, one for each state in the country. Each state has its own way of defining abuse, its own requirements for reporting it, and its own set of consequences for abusive parents.[18] Each also has its own bureaucratic standards and requirements, including its own scale of payments for foster parents. Because these differ, it is often difficult for researchers studying foster care to look at the overall nationwide picture, or to gather accurate statistics.

In many states, difficulties surround the enforcement of the laws and regulations that govern foster care. Family courts are seriously overloaded and backlogged. PL 96–272 requires a hearing to decide about permanent placement after a child has been in care for eighteen months. But today a family court judge may only have ten minutes "to determine each child's fate and each family's future," according to Paul Boland, the presiding judge of the Juvenile Courts in Los Angeles.[19] Another difficulty is the quality of the judges' decisions, or whether they are made hastily or with more consideration. In one study in the 1970s, researchers gave three family court judges the files on ninety-four children and asked the judges to decide if the children should be placed in care. These judges, who were all experienced at handling foster care cases, agreed on a decision in only half the cases. And they showed almost no agreement about why they made their decisions.[20]

A Need for Careful Thinking

Foster care does not consume a major proportion of the federal budget. Also, it does not affect millions of middle-class voters as would, for instance, changes in Social Security payments or in the tax-deductible status of mortgage interest. For these reasons, public discussion of the laws that regulate foster care is not always as intense or as informed as it might be.[21] Also, differences in city, state, and federal regulations make foster care law complicated. The lack of adequately supported family courts makes the enforcement of these laws uneven and sometimes wrongheaded.

More than one expert has made the argument that the laws regulating foster care get too little attention at the federal level. Every five or ten years Congress passes a new law that significantly affects the way in which money is distributed, and what requirements states must meet in order to get the money. To many representatives in Congress, the amount of federal dollars spent on foster care is the focus of the debate. Many of the social welfare planners who deal with foster care issues every day would like to see lawmakers give some serious consideration to the ways in which their financially based decisions affect the fundamental questions about foster care.[22]

8 Leaving Foster Care

When all is said and done, what matters most about foster care is how the children and young people who spend weeks, months, or years of their early life in foster placements get along afterward. Under what circumstances do they leave foster care? What happens to them later in their lives? There's no simple answer, because there is no one typical foster care experience. The lives that former foster children lead after they leave care differ as much as do the children themselves.

Length of Placements

Children enter foster care for a variety of reasons and stay there for periods of time ranging from a few days to an entire childhood. At one extreme, they may spend a few weeks in care during an unusual period of crisis in their families. At the other extreme, they may enter foster care from the hospital after birth and not leave until age eighteen or even twenty-one. They may have one set of foster parents, or several, or many. Having been a foster child certainly affects children's lives after they leave their foster placements. How much, and in what ways, depends on all these factors.

More than half the children who enter foster care soon return to their own homes. In 1990, for example, the average child's foster care placement lasted seventeen months.[1] Experts agree that short-term stays away from parents are not likely to have a major effect on the way children grow up.

There is a significant percentage of children who stay away from their homes for one or more years, or who never live with their biological parents again after they enter foster care. One of the largest projects ever to look closely at the experiences of children in foster care followed its subjects from their first admission through the next five years. At the end of the five-year period, 56 percent of the children had returned home. Just under 5 percent had been adopted, 3 percent were in group care, and the remaining 36 percent were still in foster homes. And of the children who were still in foster care after five years, almost 10 percent had been returned home for a part of that time—only to enter care again during the same period, some as many as three times.[2]

Statistics offer some clues as to which children are more likely to go home quickly and which may remain longer in foster care, or even grow up there. Children in Maryland who had delays or problems in development that required special educational programs were more likely to stay in foster homes for the long term. Those with parents who had physical health problems or problems with alcohol also stayed in foster care longer. Not surprisingly, those with families who were anxious to have them back spent less time in foster care. Neglected or sexually abused children remained in care twice as long as those who had been physically abused. And those who had been placed with relatives stayed with them longer than those who were in the care of strangers, which is not surprising. Caseworkers tend to see placement with a grandmother or aunt as a more natural long-term arrangement than placement with complete strangers.[3]

The earlier, larger study mentioned previously found that children who were younger when they first entered care tended to stay in care longer, while children who first entered foster homes when they were older spent less time there. One reason for this may be that older children went to foster homes from longer established relationships with their parents. The older children and their parents were used to being together, and this sense of familiarity gave momentum to their wishes to be reunited as a family.[4] This is a factor that could make adjustment to a different home even more difficult for an older foster child than for a younger one.

Older children placed because of behavior problems tend to spend less time in foster care than do younger children. Behavior problems often improve as children respond to counseling or as they become more mature. If an older child has been placed because of his or her behavior, there is some chance that the parents are not as seriously troubled as those parents whose child has been placed because of abuse and neglect. For this reason, it is more likely that the child still has a stable home to which he or she may return.

Younger children, on the other hand, more often end up in foster homes because they have been neglected or abused.[5] These are the parents' problems, and all too often the parents of children in foster care do not receive the regular services and support from the child welfare agency's overburdened caseworkers that might enable them to get their children back.

One group of children likely to return home sooner than others in foster care are those whose parents visit them regularly.[6] Staying in touch appears to be the vital ingredient in keeping the parent-child relationship alive. Sociologists and social planners point this out when they argue that the foster care system should allow for greater efforts to help the families of children in foster care. In this view, the system should offer services not just to the foster child but to the entire family. If social workers' caseloads allow them to keep in close contact with parents, the parents are more likely to visit their children. The more regularly parents visit, the more likely they are to see their families reunited.

Children who return to their original homes after they have been in foster care do not always remain there successfully. In many cases, the problems that led to their first placement recur. A child who has once been placed may well make several moves back and forth to the parental home. Caseworkers have several reasons for wanting to prevent this. In addition to the fact that they do not want children to be harmed, their agency will look bad if a child is maltreated after being released from an agency placement. Because of this possibility, caseworkers are sometimes extremely cautious about getting a family back together.[7] The caseworker may keep a child in care rather than risk a return home. Even when the child's family manages to resolve its problems, the caseworker with fifty families to supervise may be too busy to verify the improvement and bring it to the court's attention. As a result, children can experience longer than necessary stays in foster care.

While most children return home from foster care within a relatively short period of time, about a quarter of those who are placed stay in care for two years or longer.[8] And according to a study by the Black Child Development Institute, a disproportionate number of minority children remain in foster care longer than average. The study found that minority children, on average, stayed out of their homes over two years, while the average stay in placement for all children was less than a year and a half.[9]

The chances of a child returning to the original home decrease rapidly after the point at which he or she has been in care for two years.[10] When placements go on for years, foster care is more than an interruption in children's lives with their own parents. It comes to represent most, or all, of their understanding of the way people interact within families. Especially for the older child who has experienced many placements and as a result has a hard time trusting adults, adoption is as unlikely as returning home. Foster care until age eighteen is the likely life course for these young people.[11]

When Should Care End?

Many eighteen-year-olds are not ready to go out on their own, whether they have been in foster care or not. Some may still be in high school, college, or job training programs. Others may lack the skills needed to deal with people and problems that would allow them to succeed at full-time jobs and independent living. Still others, especially foster children who have been in a string of different placements, may not have family or family substitutes to fall back on if life on their own doesn't at first work out. Rich Gordon, who directs a California agency that helps youths in need, explains it this way: "The vast majority of eighteen-year-olds are not ready to live on their own in the best of circumstances. And the youngsters in foster care have never had the kind of childhood we think of as normal. They have not completed the task of being children, and yet the system demands they become independent at eighteen."[12]

Officially, though, most states define their responsibilities to children in foster care as ending when the child reaches age eighteen. In some states, the young person leaving foster care may receive a small grant to help begin independent living, but only if he or she knows about it and makes application through the agency.[13] In the mid-1980s, New York joined the list of states that now support an extended period of care. The state continues to pay foster families and to provide services to the biological parents and the foster child until he or she reaches twenty-one.[14]

Foster Children as Adults

Studies of people who spent a significant portion of their childhood in foster care suggest that in a majority of cases the experience does not deeply damage people. Two different groups of adults who grew up in foster homes were no more likely than people in general to have trouble with the law, their marriages, or mental illness.[15] A study of low-income children on the west coast over a five-year period found that foster children did not appear any more likely to suffer severe emotional disturbances than other people from the same background. Children in the same study who continued in foster care were no worse off emotionally than those who returned home.[16]

The most thorough recent study of adults who had been in foster care was the one completed in 1983 by Trudy Festinger, a professor of social work at New York University. She and her assistants interviewed a group of adults who had been in foster care in the New York metropolitan area for at least five years and who had left care when they reached eighteen.[17] The former foster children had been out of foster care for four or five years when they were interviewed.

The results of Professor Festinger's study suggest that most foster children emerge as adults who are more similar to, than different from, other people in their age group, in terms of measures like physical health and a sense of well-being.[18] The people interviewed in her study felt generally positive about their homes and neighborhoods. They had a feeling of belonging where they were living, and almost three-quarters described themselves as friendly with their neighbors. The vast majority saw themselves as having someone to count on for ad-

74

vice or help, and most felt that their lives would work out in the way they wanted. As a group, the young adults did not think of themselves first and foremost as onetime foster children.[19] Festinger summarizes, "In most instances there were no direct links . . . between factors in the past and their sense of well-being as young adults."[20]

9   Foster Care Controversies

In spite of all the changes in our society over the last 100 years, the most difficult question we face about foster care has not changed. Should social policy favor leaving children with biological parents, keeping in place what many people regard as the strongest tie that can exist between human beings? Or should it favor breaking that bond between parent and child to keep children from suffering various kinds of physical and mental damage? And should the break be temporary or permanent? So far, research and public discussion have not come up with any single definite answer.

This question really concerns the emotional well-being of a child and what factors contribute to that well-being. Child welfare agencies and parents agree that the bond between parents and their children goes far deeper than social habit. Psychologists believe that it is the model for all the other emotional connections that people form in their lives. In order for children to develop normal personalities, the ability to get along with others, and intellectual curiosity, they need a strong attachment to a parent by age five.[1]

In many cases, foster children do not develop primary bonds to adults. Foster children and foster parents both recognize their relationship as a temporary one, and tend to protect themselves emotionally by not forming strong attachments to one another.

Attachment to Foster Parents

Children who have never lived with their biological parents but who were placed with foster parents at birth, of course, have formed this crucial bond with their foster parents. In the last few years, several cases of biological parents seeking to regain custody of children in foster care since birth have generated widespread media attention. One such case arose in Chicago in 1991. Soon after she was born, Sarah was taken from her mother, a heroin addict, and placed in foster care with Joseph and Marjorie Procopio. She remained with them happily for five years. Then her birth mother, declaring she was off drugs, and the mother's boyfriend, who claims to be Sarah's father, sued for and won Sarah's custody. At first the Procopios were not even allowed to visit Sarah. They eventually gained visiting rights after a series of newspaper columns publicized the story.[2]

In a similar case in New York, Angel and Ana Rodriguez were called on to return their seven-year-old foster daughter to her mother. "Margarita" had come to them from an intensive-care ward at the hospital when she was two months old and had known no other home. While she was living with the Rodriguezes, her mother completed a drug rehabilitation program, got a job and an apartment, and regained custody of two older sons who had also been in foster care. The judge said that if a child has been voluntarily placed in care, "the government may not deprive a parent of the right to raise her child unless she is unfit to do so or in some way forfeits that right."[3]

The white foster mother of an African-American toddler, writing anonymously in the *New York Times* in 1990, told a related story from her point of view. A professional woman, "Jane Doe" had accepted the newborn son of a crack-addicted mother as a boarder baby. The idea was that she would provide him with more care and attention than he would get in a hospital. He remained with her for a year, during which time caseworkers tried to find a suitable relative or friend to take him. His biological mother entered a drug rehabilitation program but, having announced that she wanted her child back, failed on two occasions to show up to visit him. Meanwhile, the foster mother, who had become greatly attached to the boy, decided to pursue legal action. Her hope was to get the biological mother's parental rights terminated so that she might legally adopt her foster son.[4]

All three of these cases raise the same fundamental issue. Should the law favor the foster child's well-being or the rights of the child's biological parents? Family law makes it clear that natural parents have priority over foster parents, without consideration of which ones the child regards as his or her "real" or "psychological" parents. Yet removing a child who has known no other parents from a foster home and placing him or her with a person who is a stranger to the child, even though that person is a biological parent, is very likely to cause severe psychological harm. One obvious conclusion from these cases is that child welfare agencies must make every effort to develop and maintain a relationship between the child and his or her biological parents. A child who has had an ongoing relationship with biological parents will be prepared to see the family reunite, if the parents do succeed in resolving their problems. Besides, ongoing contacts might also serve to remind foster families of the possibility that their foster child may eventually return to the biological parents. It also seems clear that a foster relationship as close and important as the ones in these three cases should be able to continue. The courts and agencies should certainly allow the foster parents in such cases to visit their former foster child and keep their bond alive.

Support for Families Versus Foster Placement

Most children who enter the foster care system go from biological parents whom they know to foster parents who are strangers. Should governmental policy "tilt" toward foster care placement for these children, or toward keeping children in their own homes? One kind of experiment could help social planners decide. In this experiment, researchers would randomly divide a large group of children being considered for foster care. They would assign half to foster homes and keep half in their original homes, and then study the well-being of the two groups over time. An experiment like this might be valuable, but it would also be impossible, both morally and politically.[5]

A group of researchers in California did get a chance to research something like this. They studied children between the ages of five and ten in two neighboring California counties. One county was experimenting with giving intensive home support to families in trouble, hoping to keep the children out of foster care. The other county had no special program. The study found that, on the whole, foster care did not harm the children. Although there were individual children who seemed to get worse while in foster care, most did at least as well in school and in their emotional development as the children in the county who remained in their homes.[6]

In this California study, the researchers found some evidence that children who were more at risk of being abused and neglected benefited more from foster care than those who were at less risk. Children who stayed in their original homes had the stress of continuing difficulties. Their parents continued to abuse them to some degree, although not enough to cause serious physical injury. Children who went into foster care faced other kinds of stress. They had to go through the separation from their parents, the sadness of missing them, and the disturbing need to adjust to substitute caregivers. The researchers who conducted this study believe that foster care does not harm most children, that leaving abused children in their original homes may lead to further abuse, and that foster care may offer children from risky environments better health and more success in school.[7] But their two-year study has its limits; only a project that followed hundreds or thousands of foster children over many years could provide a definite answer.[8]

When Should Care End?

Recently, some experts have argued that if children are in foster care in their teens, they should remain in care until they reach the age of twenty-one. Groups interested in child welfare in all states are currently urging their state child welfare policymakers to raise the foster care age limit, an idea that has its drawbacks. For one thing, it would increase the number of individuals in foster care and would push up the total cost of foster care programs. But those who favor raising the age limit for foster care argue that it would be a good investment. Several recent studies suggest that a significant percentage of the foster children who are being released from care into independent living at age eighteen do not do well. Surveys of homeless people in Minneapolis revealed that 38 percent had been in foster care. Among homeless people in rural Ohio, 13 percent were onetime foster children.[9] And in a study of fifty-five people in the San Francisco Bay area who had recently left foster care at eighteen, 29 percent said they were homeless or were moving at least once a week.[10]

Simply extending the period of foster care would not, by itself, make a major difference. Trudy Festinger interviewed hundreds of adults who had spent much of their childhoods in foster care. She suggests that there be a flexible standard of age for release that would depend on a young person's maturity and whether or not he or she were still receiving education or training. She also proposes that there be a trial period of independent living before the final discharge of a foster child from care. It is important to provide foster children with very specific preparation for adult life, whether they begin it at eighteen or twenty-one. Before they go out on their own, foster children may need job counseling, training in independent living skills such as handling money, sex education and family planning information, and information about their kin and other ties.[11]

AIDS and Foster Care

As states determine whether to provide foster care services for young adults between the ages of eighteen and twenty-one, they must weigh the benfits of expanding the system. More services increase the total costs. One unavoidable expansion of services has already occurred during the last decade. The foster care system has had to take on many infants who test positive for the AIDS virus. A mother with AIDS can pass the virus to her unborn child. Sometimes the mother is too ill with AIDS, or too drug-addicted, to care for her baby when it is born. In the first few years of the AIDS epidemic, babies who tested positive for the virus often spent months in hospitals waiting for foster homes. Possible foster parents were concerned that they or their other children would catch the virus from the infants. Now that more is known about the way the disease spreads, that fear has lessened. In 1990, child welfare workers in New York City could find a foster home in two to ten days for an infant with AIDS.[12] These placements certainly allow the infants to receive more individual attention that they would get in hospitals, and they also cost the child welfare system much less. In 1990 it cost up to $6,000 a month to keep a baby with the AIDS virus in a San Francisco hospital. The top foster care payment to those taking such children into their homes was $1,729 a month.[13]

For foster parents accepting infants who have tested positive for the virus, there is reason to be hopeful. Only about one infant in three who tests HIV-positive at birth will actually develop AIDS, as explained in chapter 3. However, those who do develop AIDS usually die within two years.[14] Their foster parents need an even greater ability than the average foster parent to cope with uncertainty.

Decisions about Money

Foster care is expensive. At present, federal, state, and local governments are looking for ways to reduce their spending on social services. Researchers who study foster care issues often note that foster care might not be necessary if the same amount of money it costs to keep a child in foster care were spent to provide services to the child's family.[15] The projects that experts suggest would require coordination between different social service agencies. For instance, a city might make a serious effort to get addicted mothers off drugs while also giving them special help with raising their children. That kind of program would require the child welfare agencies to work closely with the social workers and medical personnel who deal with the problem of drug addiction. Unfortunately, interaction like this is rare in the world of city and state bureaucracy. The *New York Times* describes the system as "an array of agencies . . . sometimes working at cross-purposes, in child welfare, juvenile law enforcement, mental health, [and] public education."[16]

A related controversy concerns the way in which child welfare agencies themselves allocate funds for their activities. As the number of children in care goes up, costs inevitably increase. The current increase in numbers of foster children comes at a time when cities and states are desperately trying to cut their budgets. Agencies must make painful decisions about where the money goes and what programs to cut. In New York City in 1992, for instance, the Human Resources Administration saved $3.6 million by eliminating a ten-year-old system of evaluating foster care programs. Under that program, independent evaluation teams had rated the public and private agencies that handle the city's foster care placements. Now that the funds have been cut, the agencies will evaluate themselves by filling out questionnaires. Since these agencies receive hundreds of millions of dollars in contracts per year from the city, an independent process of evaluating their success seems like a good investment. On the other hand, the money saved will make it possible to avoid cutting the services provided directly to foster children, their biological parents, and foster families. With city and state budgets in crisis, more agencies will face difficult decisions like this one.[17]

10   Alternatives to Foster Care

As controversial as foster care is, everyone who has looked at the system agrees on a few points. One of these is that foster placement nearly always disrupts lives. Another is that it is an expensive service, costing tax-supported governmental agencies thousands of dollars per year per child. Also, some children come out of foster care with little trust in their fellow human beings, unprepared to lead happy or productive adult lives. In light of these unpleasant realities, child welfare planners are always looking for ways to change and improve the foster care programs that now exist. They also consider and experiment with alternative methods of caring for children who cannot live with their biological parents.

Family Preservation

If children can be kept safe without being placed in foster care, they avoid the stress and disruption of being removed from their homes. Child welfare policies that provide families with real help in solving their problems without placing the children in care may be able to prevent those families from breaking apart. Agencies have been legally bound to try to keep children in their own homes since the passage in 1980 of the Adoption Assistance and Child Welfare Reform Act, PL 96–272. Among other things, the law requires that states must show evidence that they have made a reasonable effort to solve problems in the home before taking children into custody. Otherwise, the states will not receive federal money to support foster care programs. The efforts that a child welfare agency might make include frequent visits from social workers with lighter than average caseloads, access to substance abuse programs, and intensive counseling with professional therapists. On the economic side, giving caseworkers special funds to help with rent, groceries, or utilities in emergencies can enable a family to get through a crisis like the loss of a job or an apartment.[1]

Programs designed to prevent foster care by helping families in their own homes are called family preservation services or intensive family support. One of the first, Homebuilders, got its start in Washington State in 1974.[2] Since then, many other states have created similar programs. Family preservation plans were being tested in Connecticut, Michigan, Missouri, New Jersey, and Tennessee in mid-1991, when New York City embarked on its version. The New York family preservation program will involve a group of caseworkers who each support only two families at a time. These workers will spend up to twenty hours per week with each family over a period of four to eight weeks. The program will cost $12 million in its first year. New York child welfare administrators hope that it will keep about 3,000 potential foster children a year in their own homes.[3]

Some intensive family support programs have produced impressive results. In Florida's Intensive Crisis Counseling Program, over 95 percent of the families who received such services avoided having their children placed in foster care. A study of Michigan's program, which served 2,400 families, found that foster placements rose by 28 percent in counties without intensive family support but fell by 10 percent in the counties that offered the program.[4] In a pilot program in the Bronx, 78 percent of the families in the program remained together a year after they had received family preservation services.[5]

Not everyone is convinced that intensive family support really works. One criticism is that the programs are more expensive than traditional social work with a family, although they are still much cheaper than foster care. In difficult budgetary times, every family cannot receive the higher level of support that the intensive programs offer. How, then, do overburdened and under-staffed child welfare agencies choose which families are at the greatest risk of losing their children to foster care? Criticizing New York's family preservation plan when it was introduced, social work professor John Schoerman said that the three careful studies of intensive support programs made to date have not shown that the programs work; other experts share his views.[6]

Helping Addicted Mothers Kick the Habit

Another new program that offers help and hope to parents who may be at risk of losing their children is currently being tried out in New York City. This program is aimed at drug-addicted mothers of newborns, most of whom have been abusers of crack cocaine. Up until the summer of 1990, child welfare workers automatically placed infants in foster care if they tested positive for illegal drugs. To get their children back, mothers had to prove that they were rehabilitated, but few managed to do so. The number of children in foster care soared, and so did the costs to the city. Under the new program, mothers can take their babies home if they are willing to agree to certain conditions.[7]

To keep their children, the addicted mothers must show an effort to get off drugs. They are required to attend drug counseling sessions and parenting classes. In addition, they must agree to have a social worker drop in on them weekly for more than a year, sometimes without warning. Some mothers resent these controls on their lives, but others find the incentive they need to get off drugs in the requirements—and in being allowed to care for their children. Program participant Gigi James said, "If they had just removed my son, I wouldn't have had anything to do but keep using drugs because I wouldn't have had my baby. When they give you the chance to keep your child, you go to the drug program. You feel it's worthwhile."[8]

High Risks, High Expectations

According to one estimate, one foster child in three who leaves foster care does not go home. Instead, these children go to more restrictive placements such as residential treatment centers, group homes, or psychiatric hospitals. The Department of Children and Youth Services in Connecticut wanted to help foster parents work with foster children who had a high risk of being institutionalized. Foster parents participating in Choice, their pilot program, attend a twelve-week intensive training session. Much is expected of these foster parents. One parent must be available to the child at all times. The parents must volunteer fifteen hours a week to the Choice network, doing things like taking foster children to appointments. In return, they get support services not available to the average foster parent. A caseworker is available to them twenty-four hours a day, and they receive a higher than average monthly payment of $1,200.

The Choice program was so successful when it was tried out in Norwich, Connecticut, that it was expanded statewide in 1991. According to a supervisor in the program, 75 percent of the foster children involved are either staying with their foster families or returning to their own families. At present the program serves only about fifty high-risk foster children yearly, but there are plans to expand it to low-risk foster children if possible.[9]

Kinship Foster Care

Another current trend in foster parenting is known as "kinship foster care." It's natural that when parents are having problems so severe that they are incapable of dealing successfully with their children, a relative of one of the biological parents should step in. Most often, the relative who does so is a woman. In New York City in 1990, 95 percent of the kinship parents surveyed were female. Kinship parents are usually close relatives of the children they take in. Grandmothers made up 67 percent of the New York group, and aunts another 22 percent.[10]

Arrangements for care by a relative often begin informally, with the relative stepping in on her own. She may then apply for official foster parent status through a child welfare agency, which will give her a monthly check to cover at least some of the expenses of having the child live with her. In order for a relative to become the official, court-approved foster parent for the child in her care, she must meet the same standards as an unrelated foster care provider. Her home must be inspected and licensed by the child welfare department before she can become eligible for a monthly stipend.

The relative often has a low or fixed income. In some cases, she may be on welfare. If so, becoming a foster parent offers her a financial advantage. Foster care payments are two to three times as great as welfare payments. In New York City in 1990, payments to foster care providers ranged from $386 to $845 a month.[11] The Supreme Court decided in 1979 that relatives providing foster care should receive the same amount as unrelated foster care providers.

Kinship foster care has proved to be an increasingly popular alternative in New York City to placement in homes with foster parents who are not related to the children. In 1985, just 151 children were placed in kinship homes. By late 1989, the total in kinship homes had mushroomed to 19,000, 42 percent of all children in care in the city.[12]

The kinship home takes advantage of naturally oc-curring ties between the child and a dependable adult often older than the child's biological parents. In the New York study, the average age of the kinship foster parents was 45.9, considerably older than the typical biological parent of a young child. Kinship foster parents tended to be stable and hard-working, and they really cared about the child.[13] Children obviously benefit by living with family members with whom they already have relationships.

There can be problems between care providers and foster children, even in a kinship home. Because so many of these children have experienced abuse, neglect, and abandonment, they can be difficult to handle, especially for the older women who most often give kinship foster care. Adequate agency support seems to be one key to making kinship foster care work. By and large, these kinship foster parents value and profit from interaction with the child welfare workers who supervise the chil-dren's cases.[14]

Foster Care and Adoption

For decades, social service professionals and foster par-ents have argued about what connection, if any, should exist between foster care and adoption. Up until the mid-1960s, child welfare agencies discouraged foster parents from adopting children in their homes who became free for adoption. In fact, this was sometimes forbidden le-gally. But in the 1960s and 1970s, foster care policy turned more and more toward the idea of permanency planning.

Having permanency as a goal meant that agencies would try, as rapidly as possible, to get children into homes where they would remain throughout childhood.

This effort would prevent children from drifting along for years in foster care. If it appeared that a child's original home would never be suitable, the agency that had the child in care would move to terminate parental rights as quickly as possible so that the child could be freed for adoption.

The mid-1960s saw a move toward a kind of half-way stage in which children who were not yet free to be adopted, but who were likely to be free in the future, were placed with families who might be interested in adopting them. These "preadoptive foster care placements" or "at-risk adoptive placements" were meant to speed up the process of getting children who would never return to their original homes into new permanent residences.[15]

All the groups involved with foster care issues, from child welfare workers to foster parents to biological parents, have raised tricky questions about foster-adoptive placements. For one thing, ending the legal relationship between biological parents and their children is a serious step indeed, at least as serious as adopting a child. The Child Welfare League of America, for one, recommends legally keeping the two procedures quite separate.[16] Also, children and foster parents who have developed strong emotional ties to one another stand to be severely hurt if the child is not eventually freed for adoption. Biological parents who have any interest in regaining custody of their children resent having them placed with families who might want to keep them. It is often difficult to determine, at the time children are placed, how likely it is that they will at some future time be able to return to their biological parents. Presently, the majority of states have some sort of foster-adoptive program.

To address the problems that have plagued traditional foster care, today's innovators in social policy are evolving imaginative alternatives. Pilot programs for caring for children in their homes, and for children at high risk of requiring institutional placement, seem likely to continue, even in the current climate of budgetary crisis. Kinship foster placements, obviously less disruptive for children than placements with strangers, are expanding nationwide. The foster-adoptive placements that are associated with the move to permanency planning will provide increased emotional security for some of the children and parents involved. For all the problems of the foster care system, important progress has been made since the days when homeless children crowded into almshouses, among the town's poorest and most hopeless citizens. The problems that are bound to arise in a system that serves people who are in many cases both underprivileged and in emotional pain must not make planners less bold. Those who have experienced foster placements, as Festinger discovered in her landmark study, are more similar to, than different from, other young Americans.[17] And no one's physical needs, emotional security, and sense of connection to the rest of humanity are more important than children's. After all, the future is in their hands.

Source Notes

Chapter 1

1. Mona Charen, "But Who Are the Real Children's Advocates?" *New York Post*, July 6, 1993, p. 18.

2. Anne Minahan, ed., *Encyclopedia of Social Work* (Silver Spring, Md.: National Association of Social Workers, 1987), Vol. 1: p. 640.

3. Minahan, pp. 641–642.

4. David Fanshel and Eugene B. Shinn, *Children in Foster Care: A Longitudinal Investigation* (New York: Columbia University Press, 1978), p. 3.

5. Jack C. Westman, *Child Advocacy: New Professional Roles for Helping Families* (New York: The Free Press [Macmillan], 1979), p. 313.

6. Trudy Festinger, *No One Ever Asked Us . . . : A Postscript to Foster Care* (New York: Columbia University Press, 1983), p. 2.

7. Mary I. Benedict and Roger B. White, "Factors Associated with Foster Care Length of Stay," *Child Welfare* 70.1 (January/February 1991), pp. 49–50.

8. Joseph Goldstein, Anna Freud, and Albert J. Solnit, *Beyond the Best Interests of the Child* (New York: The Free Press [Macmillan], 1973), pp. 98–99.

9. Gaetana Woolf, *Preparation for Fostering: A Preservice Training Manual for Foster Parents* (Plantation, Fla.: Nova University School of Social Sciences, 1987), p. 22d3.

10. Woolf, p. 22d3.

11. Leroy H. Pelton, *The Social Context of Child Abuse and Neglect* (New York: Human Sciences Press, 1981), p. 120.

12. Festinger, p. 224.

13. Festinger, p. 253.

Chapter 2

1. Susan Tiffin, *In Whose Best Interest? Child Welfare Reform in the Progressive Era* (Westport, Conn.: Greenwood Press, 1982), pp. 89–90.

2. Tiffin, p. 90.

3. Gaetana Woolf, *Preparation for Fostering: A Preservice Training Manual for Foster Parents* (Plantation, Fla.: Nova University School of Social Sciences, 1987), p. 22d2.

4. Tiffin, p. 189: quoted in David M. Rothman, *The Discovery of the Asylum: Social Order and Disorder in the New Republic* (Boston: Little, Brown, 1971), p. 157.

5. Tiffin, p. 65.

6. Andrew Billingsley and Jeanne M. Giovannoni, *Children of the Storm: Black Children and American Child Welfare* (New York: Harcourt Brace Jovanovich, 1972), pp. 33–34.

7. Woolf, p. 22d.

8. Tiffin, p. 191.

9. Billingsley and Giovannoni, pp. 33–34.

10. Billingsley and Giovannoni, pp. 27–29.

11. Tiffin, pp. 67–68.

12. Billingsley and Giovannoni, pp. 34–35.

13. Miriam Z. Langsam, *Children West* (Madison, Wis.: The State Historical Society of Wisconsin, 1964), p. 19.

14. Langsam, pp. 22–23.

15. Langsam, pp. 23–24.

16. Donald Dale Jackson, "It Took Trains to Put Street Kids on the Right Track out of the Slums," *Smithsonian Magazine*, August, 1986, p. 22.

17. Langsam, pp. 45–65.

18. Billingsley and Giovannoni, p. 70.

19. Woolf, p. 22d2.

20. Trudy Festinger, *No One Ever Asked Us . . . : A Postscript to Foster Care* (New York: Columbia University Press, 1983), p. 2.

21. Tiffin, p. 95.

22. Billingsley and Giovannoni, p. 70.

23. Robert H. Bremner, ed., *Children and Youth in America: A Documentary History* (Cambridge, Mass.: Harvard University Press, 1974), Vol. 3: p. 615.

24. Bremner, p. 614.

25. Bremner, p. 616.

26. J. C. Barden, "Foster Care System Reeling, Despite Law Meant to Help." *The New York Times*, September 21, 1990, p. 18.

27. Gilbert Y. Steiner, *The Futility of Family Policy* (Washington, DC: The Brookings Institution, 1981), p. 136.

28. Bremner, p. 623.

Chapter 3

1. National Center for Children in Poverty, *Five Million Children: A Statistical Profile of Our Poorest Young Citizens* (New York: Columbia University School of Public Health, 1990), p. 60.

2. Jack C. Westman, *Child Advocacy: New Professional Roles for Helping Families* (New York: The Free Press [Macmillan], 1979), p. 277.

3. National Center for Children in Poverty, p. 60.

4. J. C. Barden, "Foster Care System Reeling, Despite Law Meant to Help." *The New York Times*, September 21, 1990, p. 18.

5. E. Daniel Edwards and Margie Egbert-Edwards, "The American Indian Child Welfare Act: Achievements and Recommendations" in *The State as Parent: International Research Perspectives on Interventions with Young*

Persons, ed. Joe Hudson and Burt Galaway (Acquafredda di Maratea, Italy: Kluwer Academic Publishers, 1989), p. 40.

6. Barden, p. 18.

7. National Center for Children in Poverty, p. 60.

8. National Center for Children in Poverty, p. 60.

9. Barden, p. 18.

10. Deborah Daro, *Confronting Child Abuse* (New York: The Free Press [Macmillan], 1988), p. 201.

11. Leroy H. Pelton, *The Social Context of Child Abuse and Neglect* (New York: Human Sciences Press, 1981), p. 34.

12. Pelton, p. 35.

13. Barden, p. 18.

14. Monica J. Wightman, "Criteria for Placement Decisions with Cocaine-exposed Infants," *Child Welfare* 70.6 (November/December 1991), p. 654.

15. Joseph B. Treaster, "Plan Lets Addicted Mothers Take Their Newborns Home," *The New York Times*, September 19, 1991, p. 1.

16. Alessandra Stanley, "Hale House Fights City Hall for Babies' Fate," *The New York Times*, September 23, 1990, p. 38.

17. [Jane Doe], "Why Should I Give My Baby Back?" *The New York Times*, December 22, 1990, ed. page.

18. Mireya Navarro, "AIDS Children's Foster Care: Love and Hope Conquer Fear," *The New York Times*, December 7, 1990, p. B4.

19. P. A. Colón and A. R. Colón, "The Health of America's Children," in *Caring for America's Children*, ed. Frank J. Macchiarola and Alan Gartner (New York: Academy of Political Science, 1989), p. 49.

20. David Fanshel, Stephen J. Finch, and John F. Grundy, *Foster Children in a Life Course Perspective* (New York: Columbia University Press, 1990), p. 205.

21. Daro, pp. 37–38.

22. Daro, p. 39.

23. Barden, p. 18.

24. Norman Polansky, *Damaged Parents: An Anatomy of Child Neglect* (Chicago: The University of Chicago Press, 1981), p. 121.

25. Barden, p. 18.

26. Ann Rosewater, "Child and Family Trends: Beyond the Numbers," in *Caring for America's Children,* ed. Frank J. Macchiarola and Alan Gartner (New York: Academy of Political Science, 1989), p. 15.

27. Westman, p. 267.

Chapter 4

1. Michael S. Wald, J. M. Carlsmith, and P. H. Leiderman, *Protecting Abused and Neglected Children* (Stanford, Calif.: Stanford University Press, 1988), p. 63.

2. Ruth Hubbell, *Foster Care and Families: Conflicting Values and Policies* (Philadelphia: Temple University Press, 1981), p. 89.

3. David Fanshel and Eugene B. Shinn, *Children in Foster Care: A Longitudinal Investigation* (New York: Columbia University Press, 1978), p. 456.

4. Sally E. Palmer, "Group Treatment of Foster Children to Reduce Separation Conflicts Associated with Placement Breakdown," *Child Welfare* 69.3 (May/June 1990), p. 229.

5. Fanshel and Shinn, p. 456.

6. Deborah Daro, *Confronting Child Abuse* (New York: The Free Press [Macmillan], 1988), p. 81.

7. Palmer, p. 234.

8. Paul D. Steinhauer, *The Least Detrimental Alternative: A Systematic Guide to Case Planning and Decision Making for Children in Care* (Toronto: University of Toronto Press, 1991), Chapter 7.

9. David Fanshel, Stephen J. Finch, and John F. Grundy, *Foster Children in a Life Course Perspective* (New York: Columbia University Press, 1990), p. 215.

10. Fanshel, Finch, and Grundy, p. 215.

11. J. C. Barden, "When Foster Care Ends, Home Is Often the Street," *The New York Times*, January 6, 1991, p. 15.

12. Leroy H. Pelton, *The Social Context of Child Abuse and Neglect* (New York: Human Sciences Press, 1981), p. 121.

13. Fanshel, Finch, and Grundy, p. 90.

14. Celia W. Dugger, "7 Deaths in 1990 Point Up Failings of Child Protection System." *The New York Times*, January 23, 1992, p. B1.

15. Dugger, p. B5.

16. Jack C. Westman, *Child Advocacy: New Professional Roles for Helping Families* (New York: The Free Press [Macmillan], 1979), p. 315.

17. Fanshel, Finch, and Grundy, p. 206.

18. Palmer, p. 227.

19. Westman, p. 295.

20. Westman, p. 295.

21. Fanshel, Finch, and Grundy, p. 205.

22. Westman, p. 315.

23. Palmer, p. 233.

24. Fanshel, Finch, and Grundy, pp. 211–212.

25. Wald, Carlsmith, and Leiderman, pp. 86–87.

26. Trudy Festinger, *No One Ever Asked Us . . . : A Postscript to Foster Care* (New York: Columbia University Press, 1983), p. 273.

27. Festinger, p. 274.

28. Festinger, p. 275.

Chapter 5

1. David Fanshel and Eugene B. Shinn, *Children in Foster Care: A Longitudinal Investigation* (New York: Columbia University Press, 1978), p. 496.

2. Richard Weizel, "State Widens Program to Impove Foster Care," *The New York Times*, December 22, 1991, sec. 12, p. 5.

3. Weizel, p. 4.

4. Jack C. Westman, *Child Advocacy: New Professional Roles for Helping Families* (New York: The Free Press [Macmillan], 1979), p. 316.

5. Anthony N. Maluccio and Edith Fein, "An Examination of Long Term Foster Family Care for Children and Youth" in *The State as Parent: International Research Perspectives on Interventions with Young Persons*, ed. Joe Hudson and Burt Galaway (Acquafredda di Maratea, Italy: Kluwer Academic Publishers, 1989), p. 396.

6. Maluccio and Fein, p. 397.

7. Westman, p. 313.

8. Gaetana Woolf, *Preparation for Fostering: A Preservice Training Manual for Foster Parents* (Plantation, Fla.: Nova University School of Social Sciences, 1987), pp. 22e–22e2.

9. Joseph Goldstein, Anna Freud, and Albert J. Solnit, *Beyond the Best Interests of the Child* (New York: The Free Press [Macmillan], 1973), p. 24.

10. Westman, p. 313.

11. Westman, p. 317.

12. Goldstein, Freud, and Solnit, pp. 23–26.

13. Westman, p. 317.

14. Woolf, p. 36.

15. Ruth Hubbell, *Foster Care and Families: Conflicting Values and Policies* (Philadelphia: Temple University Press, 1981), p. 83.

16. Hubbell, p. 84.

17. J. C. Barden, "Foster Care System Reeling, Despite Law Meant to Help." *The New York Times*, September 21, 1990, p. 1.

18. Martin Tolchin, "Panel Seeks Foster Care Reform," *The New York Times*, February 27, 1991, p. B7.

19. Barden, p. 1.

20. Barden, p. 18.

21. Tolchin, p. B7.

22. Woolf, p. 176.

Chapter 6

1. Ruth Hubbell, *Foster Care and Families: Conflicting Values and Policies* (Philadelphia: Temple University Press, 1981), p. 110.

2. Gaetana Woolf, *Preparation for Fostering: A Preservice Training Manual for Foster Parents* (Plantation, Fla.: Nova University School of Social Sciences, 1987), p. 51.

3. Woolf, p. 51.

4. Hubbell, p. 115.

5. Woolf, p. 51.

6. Hubbell, pp. 88–89.

7. Leroy H. Pelton, *The Social Context of Child Abuse and Neglect* (New York: Human Sciences Press, 1981), p. 117.

8. Pelton, pp. 109–110.

9. Gilbert Y. Steiner, *The Futility of Family Policy* (Washington, D.C.: The Brookings Institution, 1981), p. 142.

10. Pelton, p. 117.

11. Deborah Daro, *Confronting Child Abuse* (New York: The Free Press [Macmillan], 1988), p. 200.

12. J. C. Barden, "Counseling to Keep Families Together," *The New York Times*, September 21, 1990, p. 18.

13. Katrine Ames et al., "Fostering the Family," *Newsweek*, June 22, 1992, p. 64.

14. J. C. Barden, "Washington Cedes Control of Its Foster Care Programs," *The New York Times*, July 14, 1991, p. 16.

15. Hubbell, p. 116.

16. David Fanshel, Stephen J. Finch, and John F. Grundy, *Foster Children in a Life Course Perspective* (New York: Columbia University Press, 1990), p. 219.

17. Fanshel, Finch, and Grundy, p. 2.

18. Jack C. Westman, *Child Advocacy: New Profes-*

sional Roles for Helping Families (New York: The Free Press [Macmillan], 1979), p. 301.

19. Norman Polansky, *Damaged Parents: An Anatomy of Child Neglect* (Chicago: The University of Chicago Press, 1981), p. 242.

20. Westman, p. 301.

21. David Fanshel and Eugene B. Shinn, *Children in Foster Care: A Longitudinal Investigation* (New York: Columbia University Press, 1978), pp. 498–499.

22. Fanshel and Shinn, pp. 498–499.

23. Trudy Festinger, *No One Ever Asked Us . . . : A Postscript to Foster Care* (New York: Columbia University Press, 1983), p. 280.

24. Westman, p. 301.

25. Fanshel, Finch, and Grundy, pp. 95–96.

26. Fanshel, Finch, and Grundy, p. 95.

27. Festinger, p. 287.

28. Fanshel, Finch, and Grundy, p. 202.

Chapter 7

1. Mary Jo Bane, *Here to Stay: American Families in the Twentieth Century* (New York: Basic Books, 1976), p. 112.

2. Jack C. Westman, *Child Advocacy: New Professional Roles for Helping Families* (New York: The Free Press [Macmillan], 1979), p. 311.

3. Trudy Festinger, *No One Ever Asked Us . . . : A Postscript to Foster Care* (New York: Columbia University Press, 1983), p. 41.

4. Festinger, p. 41.

5. Bane, p. 103.

6. Andrew Billingsley and Jeanne M. Giovannoni, *Children of the Storm: Black Children and American Child Welfare* (New York: Harcourt Brace Jovanovich, 1972), p. 205.

7. Deborah Daro, *Confronting Child Abuse* (New York: The Free Press [Macmillan], 1988), pp. 83–87.

8. Gilbert Y. Steiner, *The Futility of Family Policy* (Washington, D.C.: The Brookings Institution, 1981), p. 139.

9. Steiner, p. 138.

10. Daro, pp. 86–87.

11. Gaetana Woolf, *Preparation for Fostering: A Preservice Training Manual for Foster Parents* (Plantation, Fla.: Nova University School of Social Sciences, 1987), p. 22d3.

12. Woolf, p. 59.

13. Linda Greenhouse, "Suits to Speed Child Welfare Law Are Banned," *The New York Times*, March 26, 1992, p. B13.

14. Anthony N. Maluccio and Edith Fein, "An Examination of Long Term Foster Family Care for Children and Youth" in *The State as Parent: International Research Perspectives on Interventions with Young Persons*, ed. Joe Hudson and Burt Galaway (Acquafredda di Maratea, Italy: Kluwer Academic Publishers, 1989), p. 389.

15. Anne Minahan, ed., *Encyclopedia of Social Work* (Silver Spring, Md.: National Association of Social Workers, 1987), Vol. 1: p. 640.

16. Katrine Ames et al., "Fostering the Family," *Newsweek*, June 22, 1992, p. 64.

17. Maluccio and Fein, p. 389.

18. Daro, p. 19.

19. J. C. Barden, "Foster Care System Reeling, Despite Law Meant to Help." *The New York Times*, September 21, 1990, p. 18.

20. Bane, p. 106.

21. Steiner, p. 144.

22. Steiner, pp. 154–155.

Chapter 8

1. J. C. Barden, "Foster Care System Reeling, Despite Law Meant to Help." *The New York Times*, September 21, 1990, p. 18.

2. David Fanshel and Eugene B. Shinn, *Children in Foster Care: A Longitudinal Investigation* (New York: Columbia University Press, 1978), pp. 115–116.

3. Mary I. Benedict and Roger B. White, "Factors Associated with Foster Care Length of Stay," *Child Welfare* 70.1 (January/February 1991), pp. 49–50.

4. Fanshel and Shinn, pp. 116–118.

5. Fanshel and Shinn, pp. 116–118.

6. Fanshel and Shinn, pp. 98–99.

7. Gilbert Y. Steiner, *The Futility of Family Policy* (Washington, DC: The Brookings Institution, 1981), p. 142.

8. Benedict and White, p. 56.

9. Barden, p. 18.

10. Steiner, p. 138.

11. David Fanshel, Stephen J. Finch, and John F. Grundy, *Foster Children in a Life Course Perspective* (New York: Columbia University Press, 1990), p. 209.

12. J. C. Barden, "When Foster Care Ends, Home Is Often the Street," *The New York Times*, January 6, 1991, p. 15.

13. Trudy Festinger, *No One Ever Asked Us . . . : A Postscript to Foster Care* (New York: Columbia University Press, 1983), pp. 300–301.

14. Barden, p. 1.

15. Michael S. Wald, J. M. Carlsmith, and P. H. Leiderman, *Protecting Abused and Neglected Children* (Stanford, Calif.: Stanford University Press, 1988), p. 13.

16. Fanshel, Finch, and Grundy, p. 494.

17. Festinger, pp. 13–14.

18. Festinger, chs. 12–13.

19. Festinger, ch. 6.

20. Festinger, p. 126.

Chapter 9

1. Michael S. Wald, J. M. Carlsmith, and P. H. Leiderman, *Protecting Abused and Neglected Children* (Stanford, Calif.: Stanford University Press, 1988), p. 11.

2. Barbara Kantrowitz, "Children Lost in the Quagmire," *Newsweek*, May 13, 1991, p. 64.

3. "Foster Child Is Returned to Ex-addict," *The New York Times*, December 13, 1991, p. B4.

4. [Jane Doe], "Why Should I Give My Baby Back?" *The New York Times*, December 22, 1990, ed. page.

5. Mary Jo Bane, *Here to Stay: American Families in the Twentieth Century* (New York: Basic Books, 1976), p. 105.

6. Wald, Carlsmith, and Leiderman, pp. 21–24.

7. Wald, Carlsmith, and Leiderman, pp. 183–187.

8. Wald, Carlsmith, and Leiderman, pp. 182–183.

9. J. C. Barden, "When Foster Care Ends, Home Is Often the Street," *The New York Times*, January 6, 1991, p. 1.

10. Barden, p. 15.

11. Trudy Festinger, *No One Ever Asked Us . . . : A Postscript to Foster Care* (New York: Columbia University Press, 1983), pp. 299–302.

12. Mireya Navarro, "AIDS Children's Foster Care: Love and Hope Conquer Fear," *The New York Times*, December 7, 1990, p. 1.

13. J. C. Barden, "Counseling to Keep Families Together," *The New York Times*, September 21, 1990, p. 18.

14. Navarro, p. 1.

15. Jack C. Westman, *Child Advocacy: New Professional Roles for Helping Families* (New York: The Free Press [Macmillan], 1979), p. 304.

16. J. C. Barden, "Foster Care System Reeling, Despite Law Meant to Help." *The New York Times*, September 21, 1990, p. 18.

17. Celia W. Dugger, "System to Oversee Foster Care Falls Victim to Budget Cutbacks," *The New York Times*, April 20, 1992, p. 1, B6.

Chapter 10

1. Deborah Daro, *Confronting Child Abuse* (New York: The Free Press [Macmillan], 1988), pp. 81–83.

2. Celia W. Dugger, "New York City Bets Millions

on Preserving Families," *The New York Times*, July 19, 1991, p. B4.

3. Dugger, pp. 1, B4.

4. Katrine Ames et al., "Fostering the Family," *Newsweek*, June 22, 1992, p. 64.

5. Dugger, p. B4.

6. Dugger, p. B4.

7. Joseph B. Treaster, "Plan Lets Addicted Mothers Take Their Newborns Home," *The New York Times*, September 19, 1991, pp. 1, B4.

8. Treaster, p. B4.

9. Richard Weizel, "State Widens Program to Improve Foster Care," *The New York Times*, December 22, 1991, sec. 12, pp. 4–5.

10. M. A. Farber, "Mirroring New York's Ills, Kinship Foster Care Grows," *The New York Times*, November 22, 1990, p. B4.

11. Farber, p. B4.

12. Farber, p. B1.

13. Farber, p. B4.

14. Jesse L. Thornton, "Permanency Planning for Children in Kinship Foster Homes," *Child Welfare* 70.5 (September/October 1991), pp. 599–600.

15. Maryanne D. Mica and Nancy R. Vosler, "Foster-Adoptive Programs in Public Social Service Agencies: Toward Flexible Family Resources," *Child Welfare* 69.5 (September/October 1990), pp. 432–435.

16. Mica, Vosler, p. 436.

17. Trudy Festinger, *No One Ever Asked Us . . . : A Postscript to Foster Care* (New York: Columbia University Press, 1983), p. 253.

Bibliography

"Foster Child Is Returned to Ex-addict." *The New York Times* (December 13, 1991): B4.

[Doe, Jane]. "Why Should I Give My Baby Back?" *The New York Times* (December 22, 1990): editorial page.

Almeida, M. Connie, et al. "Evaluation of Foster-Family-Based Treatment in Comparison with Other Programs: A Preliminary Analysis." *The State as Parent: International Research Perspectives on Interventions with Young Persons*. Ed. Joe Hudson and Burt Galaway. Boston: Kluwer Academic Publishers, 1989.

Ames, Katrine, et al. "Fostering the Family." *Newsweek* (June 22, 1992): 64.

Bane, Mary Jo. *Here to Stay: American Families in the Twentieth Century*. New York: Basic Books, 1976.

Barden, J. C. "Counseling to Keep Families Together." *The New York Times* (September 21, 1990): 18.

Barden, J. C. "Foster Care System Reeling, Despite Law Meant to Help." *The New York Times* (September 21, 1990): 1, 18.

Barden, J. C. "When Foster Care Ends, Home Is Often the Street." *The New York Times* (January 6, 1991): 1.

Barden, J. C. "Washington Cedes Control of Its Foster Care Programs." *The New York Times* (July 14, 1991): 16.

Benedict, Mary I., and Roger B. White. "Factors Associated with Foster Care Length of Stay." *Child Welfare* 70.1 (January/February 1991): 49–50.

Billingsley, Andrew, and Jeanne M. Giovannoni. *Children of the Storm: Black Children and American Child Welfare*. New York: Harcourt Brace Jovanovich, 1972.

Bremner, Robert H., ed. *Children and Youth in America: a Documentary History*. Vol. 3. Cambridge, Mass.: Harvard University Press, 1974.

Colón, P. A. and A. R. Colón, "The Health of America's Children." In *Caring for America's Children*. Ed. Frank J. Macchiarola and Alan Gartner. New York: Academy of Political Science, 1989.

Daro, Deborah. *Confronting Child Abuse*. New York: The Free Press (Macmillan), 1988.

Dugger, Celia W. "New York City Bets Millions on Preserving Families." *The New York Times* (July 19, 1991): 1, B4.

Dugger, Celia W. "7 Deaths in 1990 Point Up Failings of Child Protection System." *The New York Times* (January 23, 1992): B1, 5.

Dugger, Celia W. "System to Oversee Foster Care Falls Victim to Budget Cutbacks." *The New York Times* (April 20, 1992): 1, B6.

Fanshel, David, Stephen J. Finch, and John F. Grundy. *Foster Children in a Life Course Perspective*. New York: Columbia University Press, 1990.

Fanshel, David, and Eugene B. Shinn. *Children in Foster Care: A Longitudinal Investigation*. New York: Columbia University Press, 1978.

Farber, M. A. "Mirroring New York's Ills, Kinship Foster Care Grows." *The New York Times* (November 22, 1990): B1, 4.

Festinger, Trudy. *No One Ever Asked Us . . . : A Postscript to Foster Care*. New York: Columbia University Press, 1983.

Goldstein, Joseph, Anna Freud, and Albert J. Solnit. *Beyond the Best Interests of the Child*. New York: The Free Press (Macmillan), 1973.

Greenhouse, Linda. "Suits to Speed Child Welfare Law Are Banned." *The New York Times* (March 26, 1992): B13.

Hubbell, Ruth. *Foster Care and Families: Conflicting Values and Policies*. Philadelphia: Temple University Press, 1981.

Jackson, Donald Dale. "It Took Trains to Put Street Kids on the Right Track out of the Slums." *Smithsonian Magazine* (August 1986): 12–22.

Kantrowitz, Barbara. "Children Lost in the Quagmire." *Newsweek* (May 13, 1991): 64.

Langsam, Miriam Z. *Children West*. Madison, Wis.: The State Historical Society of Wisconsin, 1964.

Maluccio, Anthony N., and Edith Fein. "An Examination of Long Term Foster Family Care for Children and Youth." In *The State as Parent: International Research Perspectives on Interventions with Young Persons: Report on the NATO Advanced Research Workshop on State Intervention on Behalf of Children and Youth*. Ed. Joe Hudson and Burt Galaway. Acquafredda di Maratea, Italy: Kluwer Academic Publishers, 1989.

Mica, Maryanne D., and Nancy R. Vosler. "Foster-Adoptive Programs in Public Social Service Agencies: Toward Flexible Family Resources." *Child Welfare* 69.5 (September/October 1990): pp. 432–435.

Minahan, Anne, ed. *Encyclopedia of Social Work*. Vol. 1. Silver Spring, Md.: National Association of Social Workers, 1987.

National Center for Children in Poverty. *Five Million Children: a Statistical Profile of Our Poorest Young Citizens*. School of Public Health, Columbia University, 1990.

Navarro, Mireya. "AIDS Children's Foster Care: Love and Hope Conquer Fear." *The New York Times* (December 7, 1990): 1.

Palmer, Sally E. "Group Treatment of Foster Children to Reduce Separation Conflicts Associated with Placement Breakdown." *Child Welfare* 69.3 (May/June 1990): 227–238.

Pelton, Leroy H. *The Social Context of Child Abuse and Neglect.* New York: Human Sciences Press, 1981.

Polansky, Norman. *Damaged Parents: an Anatomy of Child Neglect.* Chicago: The University of Chicago Press, 1981.

Rosewater, Ann. "Child and Family Trends: Beyond the Numbers." In *Caring for America's Children.* Ed. Frank J. Macchiarola and Alan Gartner. New York: Academy of Political Science, 1989.

Stanley, Alessandra. "Hale House Fights City Hall for Babies' Fate." *The New York Times* (September 23, 1990): 38.

Steiner, Gilbert Y. *The Futility of Family Policy.* Washington, D.C.: The Brookings Institution, 1981.

Steinhauer, Paul D. *The Least Detrimental Alternative: A Systematic Guide to Case Planning and Decision Making for Children in Care.* Toronto: University of Toronto Press, 1991.

Thornton, Jesse L. "Permanency Planning for Children in Kinship Foster Homes." *Child Welfare* 70.5 (September/October 1991): 593–600.

Tiffin, Susan. *In Whose Best Interest? Child Welfare Reform in the Progressive Era.* Westport, Conn.: Greenwood Press, 1982.

Tolchin, Martin. "Panel Seeks Foster Care Reform." *The New York Times* (February 27, 1991): B7.

Treaster, Joseph B. "Plan Lets Addicted Mothers Take Their Newborns Home." *The New York Times* (September 19, 1991): 1, B4.

Wald, Michael S., J. M. Carlsmith, and P. H. Leiderman.

Protecting Abused and Neglected Children. Stanford, Calif.: Stanford University Press, 1988.

Weizel, Richard. "State Widens Program to Improve Foster Care." *The New York Times* (December 22, 1991): sec. 12, 4, 5.

Westman, Jack C. *Child Advocacy: New Professional Roles for Helping Families.* New York: The Free Press (Macmillan), 1979.

Wightman, Monica J. "Criteria for Placement Decisions with Cocaine-exposed Infants." *Child Welfare* 70.6 (November/December 1991).

Woolf, Gaetana. *Preparation for Fostering: A Preservice Training Manual for Foster Parents.* Plantation, Fla.: Nova University School of Social Sciences, 1987.

Index

Abandonment, 62
Adoption, 11, 14, 15, 17, 27, 64, 66, 70, 73, 89–91
Adoption Assistance and Child Welfare Reform Act, 16–17, 27, 63–64, 67, 84
African-Americans, 29
Alcoholism, 30, 50, 62, 70
Aid for Families with Dependent Children (AFDC), 28, 65
AIDS, 31, 34, 82
Almshouses, 20, 21, 91

Behavior problems, 36, 71
Birtwell, Charles, 24
Black Child Development Institute, 72
Boston Children's Aid Society, 24, 25
Brace, Charles Loring, 21, 22

Case loads, 58, 72, 85
Case plans, 54–55, 56, 64–65, 66
Caseworkers, 12, 14, 15, 16, 32, 42, 43, 44, 48, 49, 50, 53–60, 66, 70, 71, 78, 82, 85, 86, 87
Casey Family Services, 57, 60
Catholics, 23
Chicago, 11, 21

Child abuse, 12, 13, 17, 19–20, 29, 30, 32–35, 36, 37, 38, 40, 41, 43, 49, 51, 52, 57, 62, 63, 67, 70, 71, 79
Children's Bureau of the United States Dept. of Labor, 25
Child protection laws, 19–20, 62, 67
Child welfare agencies, 11, 12, 13, 15, 16, 17, 25, 26, 29, 35, 42, 43, 47, 48, 49, 53, 54, 55, 57, 58, 62, 63, 65, 66, 71, 76, 78, 82, 85, 86, 89, 90
    policies of, 27, 50–51, 67
Cottage system, 25
Counseling, 12, 32, 35, 39, 55, 64, 71, 81, 85, 86
Crack cocaine addiction, 30–31, 36, 77, 86

Drug abuse, 11, 13, 30–31, 36, 50, 62, 77, 81, 86

Encyclopedia of Social Work, 13

Family courts, 62, 63, 67, 68
Family preservation, 27, 85, 86
Festinger, Trudy, 18, 74, 75, 80, 91

Foster boarding homes, 24, 25
Foster care, 60
  alternatives to, 84–91
  and custody, 15, 63
  history of, 19–27
  legal aspects of, 14–15,
    18, 35–36, 49, 53, 54,
    55, 61–68, 78, 90
  long term, 17–18, 70, 72
  multiple placements in,
    39–43
  and permanency planning,
    16–17, 27, 64, 65, 89,
    91
  and emotional stress, 37
  short-term, 15, 17, 31, 33,
    69–73
  system, 16, 18, 49, 53, 71,
    73, 79, 81, 91
Free foster homes, 21, 22,
  23–24

Group homes, 13, 26, 31, 70,
  87
Guardianship, 35, 40, 49, 62

HIV virus, 31–32, 52, 82
House Bill 96-272. See
  Adoption Assistance and
  Child Welfare Reform Act
House Select Committee
    Report on Children, Youth,
    and Families, 29

Incorrigibility, 62
Indenture, 19
Indentured servants, 19, 22

Mental illness, 11, 34, 62

National Commission on
  Family Foster Care, 51
National Foster Parents
  Association, 51

Native Americans, 29
Neglect, 11, 13, 17, 21, 23, 26,
  29, 30, 34, 35, 36, 37, 38,
  39, 40, 62, 70, 71, 79
New York, 18, 20, 21, 22, 23,
  30, 31, 57, 62, 73, 74, 81,
  83, 86, 88, 89
New York Almshouse
  Commissioners, 20
New York Children's Aid
  Society, 22, 23, 25

Orphans, 20–21, 23, 32
Orphanages, 20, 21, 24, 48
  segregated, 21

Parents,
  abusive, 32–36
  adoptive, 65
  biological, 13, 14–15, 17,
    24, 27, 33, 39–40, 42,
    43, 44, 46, 49, 51, 53,
    54, 56, 57, 60, 61, 63,
    65, 70, 74, 76, 77, 78,
    83, 84, 88, 89
  drug addicted, 30–31, 62,
    77, 82, 86–87
  foster, 11, 12, 13, 14, 16,
    18, 21, 24, 39, 43, 44,
    46–52, 53, 67, 69, 76,
    78, 81, 87, 88, 89
  ill, 31–32
  mentally ill, 11, 34, 52
  psychological, 16, 18
  rights of, 17, 27, 28, 49,
    63, 64, 90
Poorhouses, 20. See also
  Almshouses
Poverty, 24, 26, 28, 30, 31, 33,
  52, 91
Protectory, the, 23

Race, 29
Runaways, 23

Sexual abuse, 33, 36, 40, 41,
51, 52, 70
Social workers. *See*
Caseworkers
Social Security Act, 25–26
Social services, 12, 33, 35, 47,
64
Social welfare, 27
agencies, 27, 31, 49, 65

services, 25
workers, 13, 16, 17
Status offenses, 35
United States, 13, 16, 19, 27,
28, 31

White House Conference on
the Care of Dependent
Children, 24, 25